MOVING TO KELOWNA, BC

A No-Nonsense Guide

TIM YOUNG
HUGH PHILIP

Library and Archives Canada Cataloguing in Publication

Young, Tim, 1957-, author
Moving to Kelowna, BC : a no-nonsense guide / Tim N. Young, Hugh G. Philip.

Issued in print and electronic formats.
ISBN 978-0-9939822-4-8 (softcover).--ISBN 978-0-9939822-5-5 (PDF)

1. Moving, Household--British Columbia--Kelowna--Handbooks, manuals, etc. 2. Kelowna (BC)--Guidebooks. I. Philip, Hugh Graham, author II. Title.

FC3849.K36A3 2017 917.11'5 C2017-902169-9
C2017-902170-2

Published by Y2 Innovations
Cover by Ares Jun

Disclaimer: The following information is intended as a general reference guide for newcomers to Kelowna, BC. The authors, publisher and their agents assume no responsibility for any liability, loss, or risk incurred as a direct or indirect consequence of the use or application of any of the contents of this book.

All inquiries should be directed to:
Y2 Innovations c/o: www.movingtokelowna.net
Substantial discounts are offered on bulk orders of *Moving To Kelowna*. Please request details via our website.

Table Of Contents

PART TWO

IS KELOWNA A FUN AND INTERESTING PLACE TO LIVE?

PART THREE

THE ECONOMY

PART FOUR

OKAY, WHAT'S THE CATCH? . . . EVERY CITY HAS ITS CHALLENGES!

PART FIVE

BUSINESS PEOPLE YOU CAN TRUST!

INTRODUCTION

Kelowna, BC is sometimes referred to as the "Palm Springs" of Canada, and the Okanagan Valley is often referred to as the "Napa Valley of the North". If you have ever wondered what it would actually be like to live in Kelowna, or anywhere in the Okanagan for that matter, then this book will be of great value to you. *Moving To Kelowna* is not a tourist guide, although certain portions could certainly be considered as such.

Relocating to a new city can sometimes be a traumatic experience. Our goal is to provide newcomers with the objective information they will need so that their transition to Kelowna can be made with confidence.

We do this by providing facts, and a few experienced opinions, about why so many people want to live here. Being armed with no-nonsense, well-researched information will make any newcomer's transition a more stress-free, fun and enjoyable one. Cities everywhere have their pros and cons, however it is rare to have the cons exposed in order to fully enlighten potential newcomers. We include not only the benefits of moving to Kelowna, but also the challenges because we believe that being honestly informed before relocating, will not only allow for a smooth transition, but will also produce happier citizens.

Moving To Kelowna investigates these important topics and many more:

- Cost of Living Comparisons
- Home Affordability

- Weather
- Crime Levels
- Educational Opportunities
- Business Climate
- Recreational Activities
- The Local Economy and Technology Boom
- Areas for Improvement, and Some That You Will Just Have to Learn to Live With

The authors are two enthusiastic but realistic residents who have enjoyed life in Kelowna for more than 25 years. We have raised our families here, operated our businesses here, and we plan to retire here.

We close our publication with the best business referrals that we could muster. These are trusted business people that will help you settle in once you arrive; and, they will give you a discount, to boot!

If you want to make the most informed decision you can before relocating to Kelowna, then *Moving To Kelowna* is arguably the most convenient and valuable investment you can make.

PART ONE

Interesting Facts And Stats

"LIES, DAMNED LIES, AND STATISTICS."
BENJAMIN DISRAELI

CHAPTER 1

HISTORY OF KELOWNA

The Syilx were the valley's first people believed to have migrated from the north over 10,000 years ago. They were self-reliant hunter-gatherers of food, clothing and shelter, who flourished throughout the region.

The first foreigners to visit the Kelowna area were the fur traders who traveled the Brigade Trail between Fort Vancouver (present day Vancouver, Washington) up through central Washington and the Okanagan Valley to Fort Kamloops in the early 19th century. The trail linked to others that led to the gold fields in the Fraser Canyon and the Cariboo region of central BC where many miners from the US and Europe sought their fortunes.

Father Charles Pandosy

1859 saw the arrival of the first European settlers in the Okanagan Valley - Father Charles Pandosy, Father Richard, and Brother Surel, from Marseilles, France via the US. They established a mission in Kelowna that eventually included a school and later farm outbuildings. Father Pandosy is credited with planting the first apple tree in the Okanagan Valley and planting the first vineyard for the production of sacramental wine. Today the Father Pandosy Mission is a BC Heritage Site which is open to the public.

Once the town planners had laid out the town site in 1892, it needed a name. Legend has it that a group of returning Syilx hunters came across an early settler, August Gillard, emerging from his semi-underground 'soddy' dwelling. They called out 'Kim-ach-Touch, Kim-ach-Touch' which means 'Brown bear, Brown bear' because of Albert's fur coat and whiskered appearance. Town planners considered Kim-ach-Touch as a possible town name. However people had trouble pronouncing the name and so they settled on 'Kelowna', derived from the Okanagan First Nation's name for "grizzly bear".

Kelowna was incorporated on May 4, 1905 when it had a population of 600.

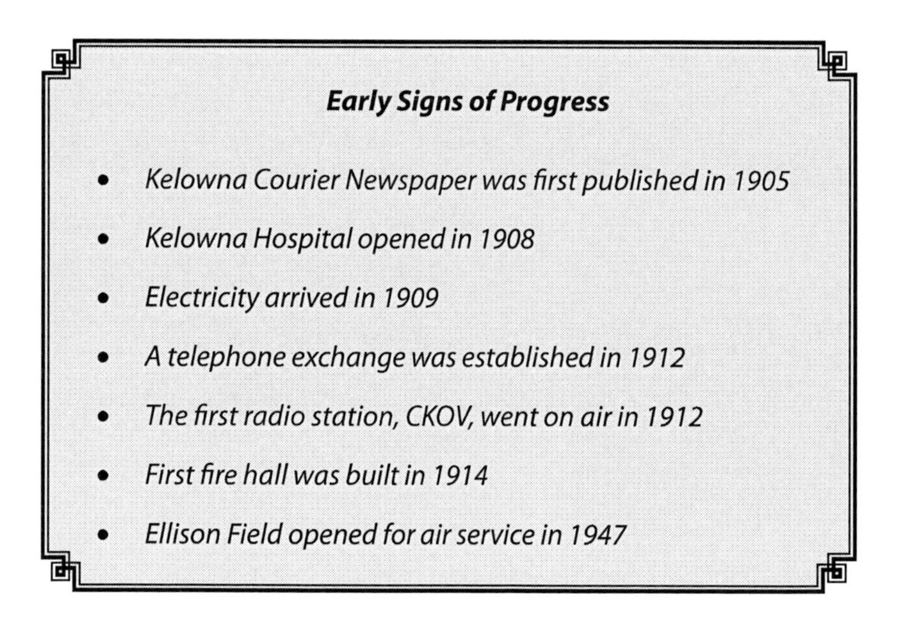

Early Signs of Progress

- *Kelowna Courier Newspaper was first published in 1905*
- *Kelowna Hospital opened in 1908*
- *Electricity arrived in 1909*
- *A telephone exchange was established in 1912*
- *The first radio station, CKOV, went on air in 1912*
- *First fire hall was built in 1914*
- *Ellison Field opened for air service in 1947*

The community of Rutland, just northeast of Kelowna, appeared around 1908. Another neighbouring community, South (Okanagan) Mission, developed south of Kelowna at about the same time. In 1973 the City of Kelowna boundaries were expanded to include Rutland, Okanagan Mission and surrounding farm land by an act of the provincial legislature. The boundary expansion did not include the unincorporated area on the west side of the lake that included the distinct neighbourhoods of Westbank, Shannon Lake, Glenrosa, Casa Loma, West Kelowna Estates, Rose Valley and Lakeview Heights. This area was officially incorporated as the District of West Kelowna on December 6, 2007 after residents narrowly passed a referendum to create the district in June 2007.

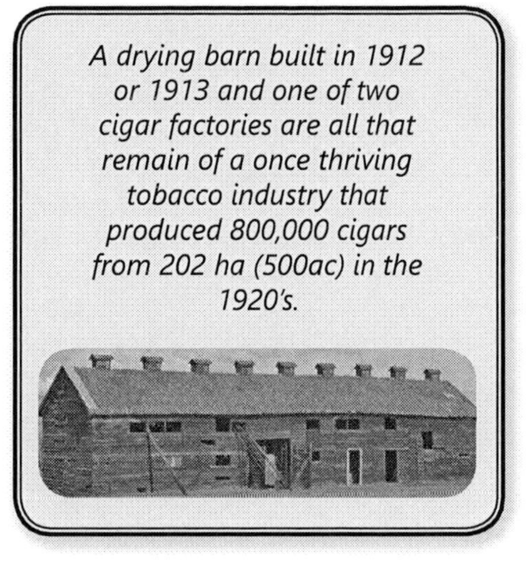

A drying barn built in 1912 or 1913 and one of two cigar factories are all that remain of a once thriving tobacco industry that produced 800,000 cigars from 202 ha (500ac) in the 1920's.

Tobacco and hay production were gradually replaced by tree fruit production, and established the area as a major apple and pear production region in Canada. The industry became a major employer not only in the orchards but also in the many packinghouses and businesses established to support the growers.

The BC Fruit Growers' Association, headquartered in Kelowna, was created in 1892 to represent the interests of valley tree fruit growers and to help the industry innovate and be competitive. In 1946, local fruit growers created BC Fruit Processing Ltd. to produce a 100% pure apple juice, made with apples straight from the orchard. They named the new juice "SunRype" which became the name of a respected and popular producer of fruit drinks and related products marketed around the world.

Soon after the completion of the Canadian Pacific mainline in 1893, a spur line was built to Okanagan Landing west of Vernon. From here passengers and goods would transfer to stern wheel steamers and other water craft to continue their trip to Kelowna and communities further south. The first stern wheel steamer to begin service on the lake was the S.S. Aberdeen. Built in 1893, the Aberdeen could carry 250 passengers and up to 180 tonnes of cargo. It was decommissioned in 1916.

In 1925, the Canadian National Railway arrived in Kelowna connecting the city to Vernon and Kamloops. Although lake steamers were no longer needed, the ferry service continued between Kelowna and Westbank until construction of the 1.4 km (0.8 mi.) long Okanagan Lake Bridge in 1958. Railway service between Vernon and Kelowna ended in 2013 and plans are underway to convert the abandoned rail bed into a recreational trail connecting the two cities.

The Kettle Valley Railway was completed in 1915, linking Vancouver and the Kootenays and providing Okanagan fruit growers access to foreign markets. Starting in 1961 portions of the rail line were gradually abandoned until the final segment was removed in 1989. Much of the old rail bed is now a multi-use recreational trail known as the Kettle Valley Rail Trail. One of the most popular sections of the trail is in the Myra-Bellevue Provincial Park. This section has 18 trestles and two tunnels that attract thousands of locals and tourists every year.

More information on the history of Kelowna, the Okanagan and the interesting personalities involved is available in the published annual reports of the Okanagan Historical Society.

CHAPTER 2

LET'S GET OUR BEARINGS

The City of Kelowna is located in the province of British Columbia, the most westerly of the ten provinces in Canada. It is situated on the east side of Okanagan Lake about midway along the length of the lake (Figure 1). The city is in the Pacific Standard Time (PST) zone (UTC/GMT difference, -08:00 h) and observes daylight saving time (2nd Sunday in March to 1st Sunday in November).

Geographic coordinates for Kelowna:

- *Latitude: 49°53'16.74" N (49.8830700°)*
- *Longitude: 119°29'45.61" W (19.4856800°)*
- *Elevation above sea level: 355 m (1165 ft.)*

The city is bordered east and west by tree-covered mountainous hills which rise more than 1,000 m above Okanagan Lake.

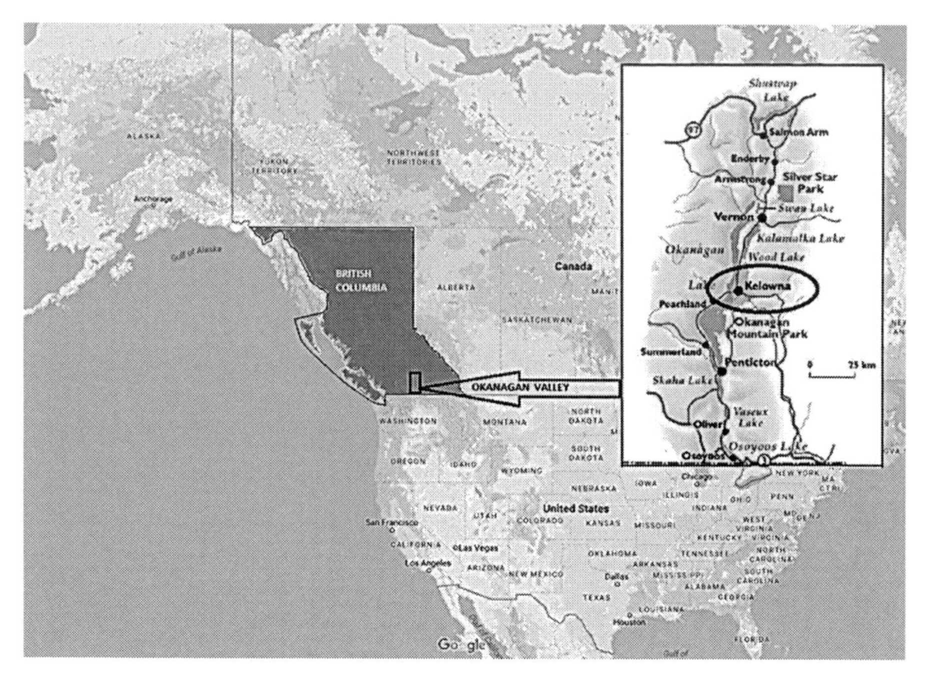

Figure 1. Location of Kelowna, BC. Courtesy Google Maps.

Table 1 shows the approximate driving and flight travel distances and times from Kelowna to major Canadian and US cities, and two Mexican holiday destinations. Of course the distances and times vary according to the flight/route you take and the number of stops along the way.

Table 1. Driving (non-stop) and flight (* 1 stop) travel distances and times from Kelowna.

City	Air Travel		Driving	
	Distance (km)	Time (h)	Distance (km)	Time (h)
Vancouver, BC	270	0.6	390	4.0
Calgary, AB	405	0.75	603	6.75
Edmonton, AB	580	1.2	893	9.3
Regina, SK	1061	4.75*	1375	13.75
Winnipeg, MB	1596	4.3*	1945	19.3
Toronto, ON	3094	4.25	4052	37.75

Ottawa, ON	3271	6.5*	3956	41.25
Halifax, NS	4161	6.5*	5392	54.6
Seattle, WA	328	1.0	500	5.0
Los Angeles, CA	1764	5.25*	2329	22
Phoenix, AZ	1926	8.25*	2449	24
Palm Springs, CA	1801	6*	2340	23.5
Cancun, MX	4288	6.5	6314	65
Puerto Vallarta, MX	3487	5.0	4323	46

Figure 2 shows that Highway 97 is the only major north-south highway connection to Kelowna. US Hwy 97 starts 1067 km (663 mi.) south in Weed, California and passes through our city as Harvey Avenue. It continues north for 2081 km (1299 mi.) to end in Watson Lake, Yukon, where it joins the Alaska Highway.

The only highway heading east from our city is BC Hwy 33. It leaves Hwy 97 heading southeast to join BC Hwy 3 which forms the southern route into Alberta (AB) through the Crowsnest Pass. Hwy 3 ends in Medicine Hat, AB where it joins the Trans-Canada Hwy 1.

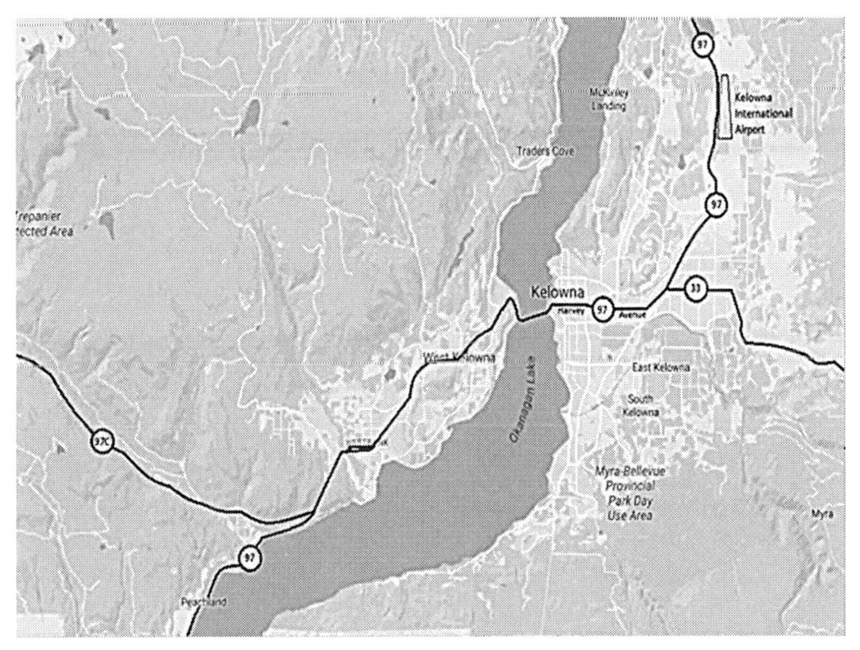

Figure 2. Highways serving Kelowna and area.

Highway travel to Vancouver begins just south of West Kelowna where the Coquihalla Connector (Hwy 97C) joins Hwy 97. The Connector ends 224 km (139 mi.) west at Merritt where it joins the Coquihalla Highway (Hwy 5). This highway links Kamloops in the north to Hope in the south, forming an alternate and faster route than the Trans-Canada Hwy 1 from Kamloops to Hope, and on to Vancouver.

CHAPTER 3

WHO ARE WE SO FAR? DEMOGRAPHIC ANALYSIS

Potential newcomers may be interested to learn about who currently lives in Kelowna, and how we compare to other parts of Canada, from a demographic perspective. Is it true that Kelowna is mostly made up of English speaking wealthy senior citizens? We'll let the facts speak for themselves and leave the conclusions to you.

There are reams of demographic data produced by our friends at Statistics Canada, however we have tried to glean from this information where Kelowna might be notably different from other locations which may help define who we are. Unless otherwise stated, the information in this chapter is from Statistics Canada (StatsCan CANSIM Tables).

Statistics can be confusing at times, especially when the definitions and/or geographic boundaries change. It is important for readers to understand the difference between a reference to **City of Kelowna** (Fig. 1) and a reference to the **Kelowna CMA (Census Metropolitan Area)** (Fig. 2). A reference to Kelowna means the people and lands within the legal city boundary. A reference to the Kelowna CMA includes the city of Kelowna **and** the surrounding communities of West Kelowna, Lake Country and Peachland.

For the most part, we will provide data comparing the Kelowna CMA to other CMAs in Canada. The reason for this is because CMA data is the most accurate and readily available source of information used for such comparative purposes.

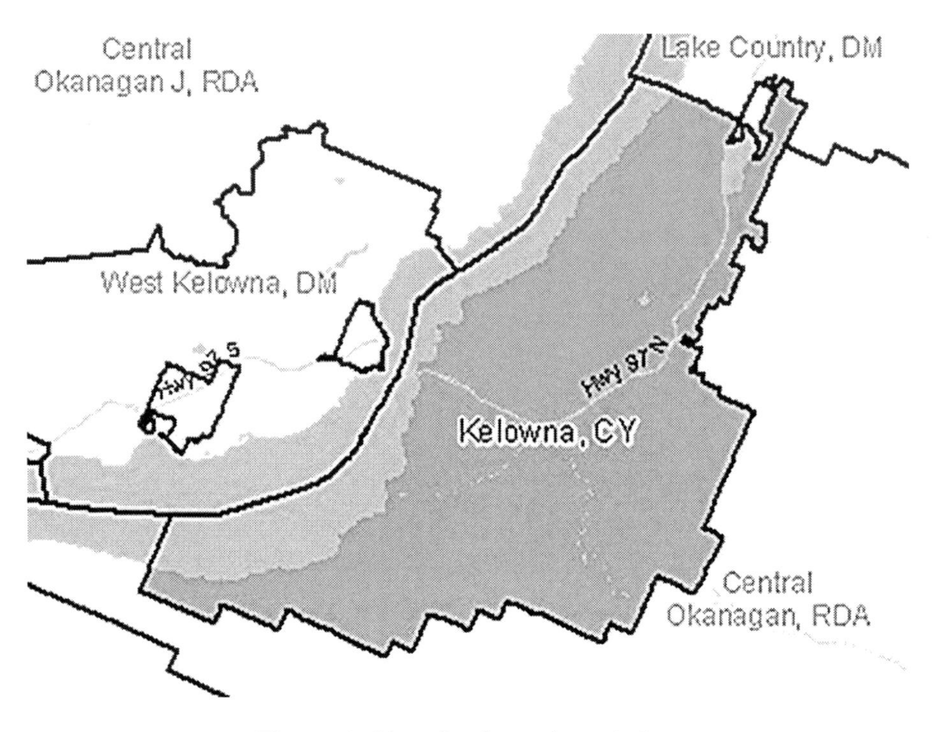

Figure 1. City of Kelowna boundaries.

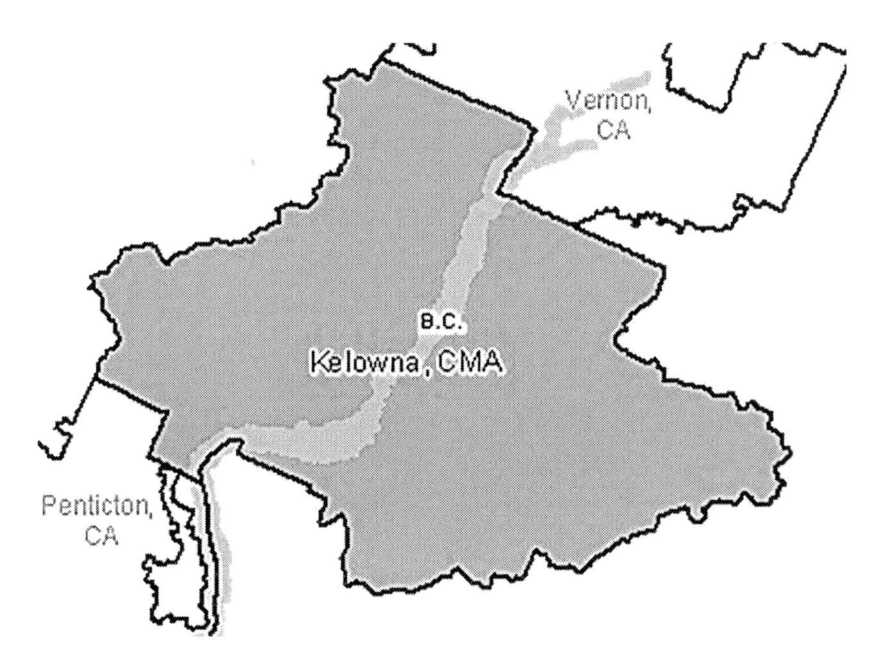

Figure 2. Kelowna CMA (Census Metropolitan Area).

1. Quick Facts

Table 1. Comparative population statistics.

		Canada
Population City of Kelowna	127,380	35.1 mil
Population of Kelowna Census Metropolitan Area (CMA)	194,882	N/A
Population Rank Among all CMA's in Canada	22	N/A
Provincial Population Rank Among CMA's in BC	3	N/A
Population Growth Rate (2011-2016)	8.4%	5.0%
Growth Rate Rank (2011-2016) Among all CMA's in Canada	6	N/A
Per Cent of Population Over 65 Years	21.4	16.9
Median Age of Population (Years)	45.5	41.2

Source: Statistics Canada 2016 Census.
Catalogue no. 98-316-X2016001. Ottawa. Released October 25, 2017.

Kelowna CMA ranked fourth highest (21.4%) among the 35 CMAs across Canada for the proportion of the population aged 65 and over.

2. Income & Wealth

Table 2. Comparison of Kelowna CMA median household income and tax filer investment income to BC and Canadian levels.

	Kelowna	BC	Canada
Median Total Household Income, 2015[1]	$71,127	$69,995	$70,336
Median Investment Income of Tax Filers, 2015[1,2]	$1,070	$830	$660

[1]Source: Statistics Canada.
[2]Investment income recipients are defined as tax filers who either reported dividend income from taxable Canadian corporations or reported interest income. Income earned from investments held under the terms of registered retirement savings plans or registered retirement income funds, for example, are excluded. Capital gains are also excluded.

Table 3 illustrates the relative wealth of families by Province, and how that has changed over time. We wonder if this data reveals why some suggest that BC means 'Bring Cash' rather than British Columbia?

Table 3. Median net worth of families and changes 2012 - 2016.

	Net Worth[1]	% Change
British Columbia	429,400	18.3
Ontario	365,700	30.5
Manitoba	320,800	35.2
Saskatchewan	293,500	2.5
Alberta	290,500	2.9
Nova Scotia	225,200	11.0
Newfoundland	211,800	19.6
Quebec	208,900	0.0
Prince Edward Island	204,000	28.6
New Brunswick	158,400	-14.2
Canada	295,100	14.7

[1]All dollar amounts are in constant 2016 dollars
Source: Statistics Canada. *Survey of Financial Security.*

Table 4 shows how the median family income of the Kelowna CMA compares to that of other Canadian CMAs.

Table 4. Change in median total income of households of census families between 2005 and 2015.

CMA	2005	2015	% Change
Calgary	81,138	99,583	22.7
Edmonton	74,615	94,447	26.6
Regina	65,897	84,447	28.1
Saskatoon	60,856	82,999	37.0
Ottawa-Gatineau	78,645	82,052	4.3
Guelph	79,225	81,223	2.5
St. John's	62,554	79,750	27.5
Toronto	75,862	78,373	3.3
Vancouver	65.342	72,662	11.2
Kelowna	**59,517**	**71,127**	**19.5**
Winnipeg	60,719	70,795	16.6
Canada	63,457	70,336	10.8
Victoria	63,057	70,283	11.5
Halifax	64,002	69,522	8.6
Quebec	58,815	65,359	11.1
St. John	58,038	63,737	9.8
Montreal	56,771	61,790	8.8

Source: Statistics Canada. 2017. *Focus on Geography Series, 2016 Census.*

If one believes that investment income is a legitimate indicator of personal wealth, then the information provided in the next few paragraphs and Table 5 should prove to be quite enlightening. Investment income recipients are defined by Statistics Canada as tax filers who either reported dividend income from taxable Canadian corporations or reported interest income. Income earned from investments held under the terms of registered retirement savings plans or registered retirement income funds, for example, are excluded. Capital gains are also excluded. In other words, the higher the investment income, the higher the wealth of an individual.

According to the Statistics Canada 2016 Census, tax filers in Alberta reported the highest median investment income ($840), followed by those in British Columbia ($830) and Saskatchewan ($720). Tax filers in Nunavut ($210) reported the lowest median investment income, followed by those in Newfoundland and Labrador ($330) and the Northwest Territories ($340).

Among Census Metropolitan Areas (CMAs), Victoria ($1,100) reported the highest median investment income among tax filers, followed by Kelowna ($1,070) and Calgary ($1,000). The Victoria CMA also had the highest proportion of tax filers reporting investment income at 37.8%, followed by Kelowna and Vancouver (both at 36.6%).

Table 5. 2015 Annual median investment income $ by CMA.

CMA	$
Victoria	1100
Kelowna	**1070**
Calgary	1000
Vancouver	840
Edmonton	740
Saskatoon	730
Halifax	710
Toronto	710
Regina	680
Canada	660
Montreal	600
Abbotsford	560
Quebec	540
Winnipeg	500
Saint John	480
Moncton	430
St. John's	380

Source: Statistics Canada CANSIM table 111-0038.

3. Language

In the 2016 Kelowna CMA Census, 85.8% of the population reported English only as their mother tongue, 1.6% reported French only, and 11.6% reported only a non-official language. All three remained essentially unchanged from the 2011 census. In comparison, the BC percentages were 68.9% for English only, 1.2% for French only and 27.6% for only non-official languages.

The 2016 Census also revealed that English was spoken most often at home by 94.0% of the Kelowna CMA population, 0.4% spoke only French and 3.6% spoke only a non-official language. In comparison, the BC percentages were 79.0% for English only, 0.4% for French only and 15.6% for only a non-official language.

Table 6. Most common non-official language mother tongues in Kelowna[1].

Mother Tongue	Number	Percentage of Non-Official Language Mother-tongue Population	Percentage of Total Kelowna Population
German	4,270	23.3	2.8
Panjabi (Punjabi)	1,655	9.0	1.1
Chinese languages	1.285	7.0	0.8
Tagalog (Pilipino, Filipino)	940	5.1	0.6
Spanish	885	4.2	0.6
Dutch	780	4.2	0.5
Ukrainian	730	4.0	0.5
Italian	730	4.0	0.5
Polish	640	3.5	0.4
Russian	620	3.4	0.4
Japanese	360	2.0	0.2
Arabic	285	1.5	0.2

[1] Excluding institutionalized residents.

Source: Statistics Canada. 2017. Kelowna [Population centre], British Columbia and Canada [Country] (table). Census Profile. 2016 Census. Statistics Canada Catalogue no. 98-316-X2016001. Ottawa.

4. Religious Affiliations

Please see Chapter 17 for a detailed discussion of this topic.

5. Immigrant Population

According to the 2016 National Household Survey (NHS), 26,450 (13.9%) of the population of the Kelowna CMA were foreign-born (immigrants), 162,955 (85.0%) were Canadian-born (non-immigrants) and 2,055 (1.1%) were non-permanent residents.

One question arose as we reviewed the 2016 census immigration data was: How does the Kelowna CMA compare to other CMAs as a destination for immigrants? The next question was: How can we compare CMAs? Currently the number of immigrants settling in cities is used to compare desirability of cities. But this is unfair to smaller cities and towns as they cannot compete with the attraction of large urban centres. To overcome this bias, we calculated a relative ratio as follows:

$$\frac{\text{\% of CMA's population made up by immigrants}}{\text{\% of Canada's population made up by the CMA}}$$

Where the ratio is 1.0, the immigrant portion of a CMA's population is the same proportion as the CMA's share of the total national population. The higher the value (>1.0), the more relatively attractive the CMA; the lower value (<1.0), the less relatively attractive the CMA.

Table 7 presents the results of our analysis. The results confirm that, in general, more immigrants are settling in the larger cities (>300,000, except for Quebec City and Halifax) based on the proportion of immigrants. However, when relative ratios are compared, the range differences among CMAs is less dramatic. For example, the immigrant portion of the Toronto CMA population (35.8%) is many times greater than that of Kelowna's CMA (0.4%). However, when relative ratios are compared, Kelowna CMA's share is only 66.7% less than the Toronto CMA. For Kelowna to achieve a relative ratio of 1.0, Kelowna would have to welcome about 20,000, or 75%, more immigrants.

In comparison, the proportion of the population of BC who were immigrants was 28.3%, 69.5% were non-immigrants, and 2.2% were non-permanent residents. In terms of Canada as a whole, 22% were immigrants and 78% were Canadian-born.

Table 7. Relative ratio of immigrant population.

CMA	Total Population	%	Number of Immigrants[1]	%	Relative Ratio
Canada	35,151,728	100	7,540,830	21.4	
Toronto	5,928,040	16.9	2,705,550	35.8	2.1
Vancouver	2,463,431	7.0	989,940	13.1	1.9
Calgary	1,392,609	4.0	404,700	5.4	1.4
Montreal	4,098,927	11.7	936,305	12.4	1.1
Edmonton	1,321,426	3.8	308,605	4.1	1.1
Winnipeg	778,489	2.2	181,965	2.4	1.1
Hamilton	747,545	2.1	177,070	2.3	1.1
Ottawa	1,323,783	3.8	255,800	3.4	0.9
Victoria	367,770	1.0	65,610	0.9	0.9
Saskatoon	295,095	0.8	45,155	0.6	0.8
Regina	236,481	0.7	36,910	0.5	0.7
Kelowna	**194,882**	**0.6**	**26,450**	**0.4**	**0.7**
Halifax	403,390	1.1	37,205	0.5	0.4
Quebec City	800,296	2.2	44,550	0.6	0.3
St. John's	205,955	0.6	8,135	0.1	0.2
Saint John	126,202	0.4	6,645	0.1	0.2

[1]'Immigrants' includes persons who are, or who have ever been, landed immigrants or permanent residents prior to May 10, 2016.
Source: Statistics Canada. 2017. *Focus on Geography Series, 2016 Census*. Statistics Canada Catalogue no. 98-404-X2016001. Ottawa, Ontario. Analytical products, 2016 Census.

The three most common countries of birth of immigrants living in the Kelowna CMA were:

- United Kingdom (21.0%)
- Germany (10.7%)
- United States (7.7%)

In comparison, the top three countries of birth of immigrants living in British Columbia were:

- China (15.5%)
- India (12.6%)
- United Kingdom (9.6%)

6. Visible Minorities

Table 8. Comparison of visible minority populations in Kelowna to Canada as a whole (2016).

	Kelowna CMA	% of Total Pop.	Canada	% of Total Pop.
Total population	194,882	100	35,151,728	100
Visible minority population	14,930	7.8	7,674,580	22.3
South Asian	3,925	2.1	1,924,635	5.6
Chinese	2,340	1.2	1,577,060	4.6
Black	1,260	0.7	1,198,545	3.5
Filipino	1,885	1.0	780,125	2.3
Latin American	1,065	0.6	447,325	1.3
Arab	300	0.2	523,235	1.5
Southeast Asian	775	0.4	313,260	0.9
West Asian	390	0.2	264,305	0.8
Korean	630	0.3	188,710	0.5
Japanese	1,580	0.8	92,920	0.3
Visible minority, not included elsewhere	285	0.1	132,090	0.4
Multiple visible minority	505	0.3	232,375	0.7
Not a visible minority	175,630	92.2	26,785,480	77.7

Source: Statistics Canada, 2016 Census. Catalogue no. 98-404-X2016001.

7. Aboriginal Population

Please see Chapter 18 for a detailed discussion of this topic.

8. Changes to In-Migration

For many years Kelowna has been described as a retirement community. The facts from the 2016 Census seem to support this long held theory, as the Kelowna CMA does have a higher percentage of people over the age of 65 than does the national average.

There is a new theory being bantered about the streets of Kelowna, particularly from downtown residents employed in the burgeoning high tech sector. There are those who believe that newcomers to Kelowna are no longer seniors looking for rest and relaxation. They suggest that today's newcomers are predominantly young millennials looking for work in the tech industry, and young entrepreneurs seeking a life-style improvement. At present, there is little statistical data to support this claim, however anecdotal support abounds.

Regardless of age, there are a number of options for newcomers to learn about what it's really like to live in the Kelowna area. One such option is to join the Kelowna Newcomers' Club (KNC). This club is a non-profit, activities-based social group designed to help newcomers meet people and make new friends. To be eligible, you must have lived in Kelowna for less than 3 years and be at least 18 years of age. The cost of membership is only $25.00/year. Visit kelownanewcomers.ca to discover more than over 20 available activities.

CHAPTER 4

WHAT THE HECK IS THE RDCO?

When people first visit Kelowna, they may get the impression that the whole area is one jurisdiction. The fact is the City of Kelowna is a member of a larger jurisdiction – the Regional District of Central Okanagan (RDCO). This is important to know because the availability and cost of housing and utilities can vary according to the jurisdiction in which you settle.

The RDCO was created in 1969 and is one of 29 regional districts in BC. Regional Districts (RDs) are similar to counties, regional municipalities or other intermediate regional levels of government between local (towns, cities) and provincial governments.

The concept of regional districts emerged in the early 1960's when population growth in BC was increasing rapidly due to resource development. The growing rural populations had no general purpose local government but relied on the provincial government to regulate and provide the services. In 1965 the provincial *Municipal Act* was amended to provide for the incorporation of regional districts and 29 regional districts were created over the next 5 years.

The RDCO is made up of two unincorporated electoral areas (Central Okanagan West and Central Okanagan East) and four member self-governed municipalities (City of Kelowna, District of West Kelowna, District of Peachland, and District of Lake Country (Fig. 1)).

The self-governed Westbank First Nation's (WFN) reserve lands are the black areas identified with IR# in Figure 1. The RDCO headquarters are in Kelowna. The four member municipalities also comprise the Kelowna Census Metropolitan Area. The RDCO is the third largest of 29 RDs in the area (2,905 km^2 or 1,121 mi^2) and has the 4th largest population in BC.

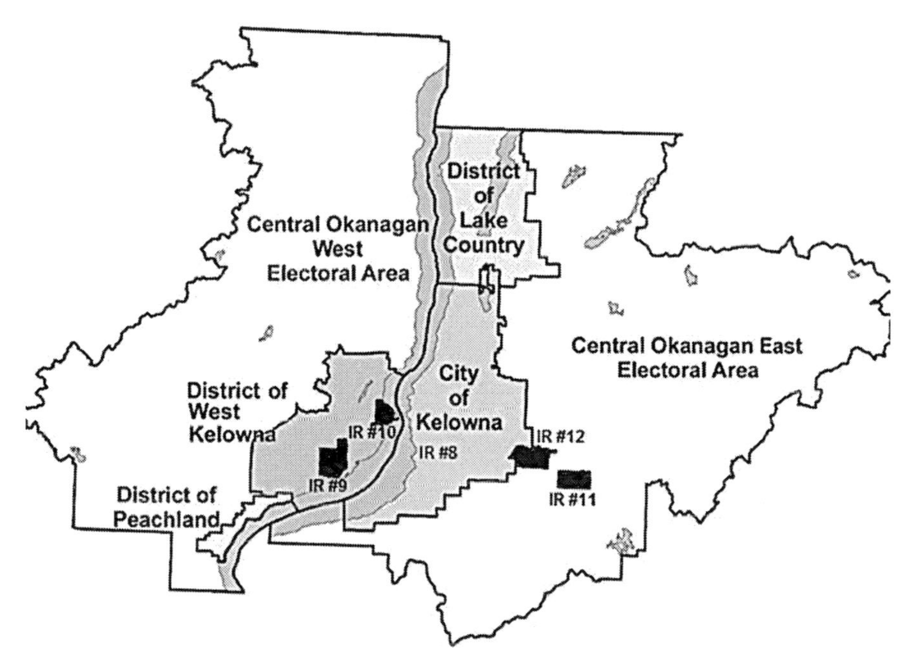

Figure 1. Member Municipalities and Electoral Areas in the Regional District of Central Okanagan and Westbank First Nation's Indian Reserves (IR) 8-12.

The governance activities of the RDCO are funded by taxes collected annually by the province and member municipalities and the electoral areas. Some residents also pay for services directly, such as water and garbage. The total 2017 budget was $64.7 million, and the average RDCO tax on a Kelowna home valued at $594,000 in 2017 was $176.52. Of course, this is in addition to the taxes Kelowna residents pay for the services provided by the City of Kelowna.

The RDCO is governed by a Board of Directors comprised of 12 voting members, ten of which are appointed from their respective member municipal councils (including the mayors), and two are elected by their electoral area constituents. The Westbank First Nation has one non-voting member to represent the interests of its Council and members.

The RDCO enacts and enforces bylaws that dictate how the RDCO conducts its in-house business, as well as the services it delivers to citizens. In some cases the RDCO enforces bylaws on behalf of its member municipalities to provide a regional approach to enforcement services. The RDCO provides:

- Basic services such as: recreation, park facilities, fire protection, and garbage collection to homes and businesses located within the electoral areas.
- Regional services such as 911, dog control, noxious insect and weed control, mosquito control, parks and recycling for both the member municipalities and electoral areas.
- Wastewater treatment services for the City of West Kelowna, District of Peachland and Westbank First Nation.
- Administration for 50 regional parks.

The RDCO operates six water systems to provide potable water to about 959 customers, and services the sewer system and operates a wastewater treatment plant for West Kelowna, Peachland and Tsinstikeptum Indian Reserves 9 and 10.

The Waste Reduction Office oversees regional curbside recycling, garbage and yard waste collection for **all** residents and businesses in the RDCO using colour-coded collection bins that are emptied weekly (garbage) or bi-weekly (recycling, yard waste) and taken to one of two regional disposal sites.

The Central Okanagan Economic Development Commission (COEDC) is the RDCO's primary business resource. It facilitates economic growth by supporting local businesses, and attracting new people, companies and investment.

Another important advisory body the RDCO established is the Environmental Advisory Commission. Its mandate is to advise the RDCO Board on the environmental aspects of land use planning and impact on environmental sustainability.

In 2016 there were 879 farms in the RDCO that produced almost 20 different crops and 14 different kinds of livestock and poultry. This generated $120.2 million in total gross farm receipts.

In 1970 the RDCO, in collaboration with the other three Okanagan RDs, established the Okanagan Basin Water Board to provide leadership on water issues spanning the valley. Local governments have enacted bylaws designed to conserve water (e.g. prohibited certain uses, year-round watering restrictions, and approval of domestic irrigation systems). The public is becoming more engaged in proper watering, designing landscaping needing less water, and installing water saving fixtures.

In recent years, questions have been raised about the need for Regional District governments when most of the population live in municipal jurisdictions. In the Okanagan, some question why there are three RDs when one could deliver the same services throughout the Okanagan and Similkameen valleys at less administrative cost. With so many joint boards and commissions advising the RDs, it is not unreasonable to foresee such an amalgamation.

CHAPTER 5

THE ALR CONTROVERSY?

This chapter involves a subject that continues to create some controversy since its creation with the passing of BC's *Land Commission Act* in 1973. We will attempt to clarify the controversy by describing what the legislation created, the main issues identified by each side, and how you can avoid coming in conflict with either side.

The *Land Commission Act* allowed the establishment of a special land-use zone, the Agricultural Land Reserve (ALR), in which agriculture is recognized as the priority use. Farming is encouraged and non-agricultural uses are restricted. The Agricultural Land Commission, established at the same time, was tasked to preserve BC farmland, encourage farming, and to work with local governments to achieve these objectives.

What this meant is that ALR land could not be sold for non-agricultural purposes or sub-divided unless expert opinion deemed the land unsuitable for agriculture, or that the proposed development would not impede agricultural production.

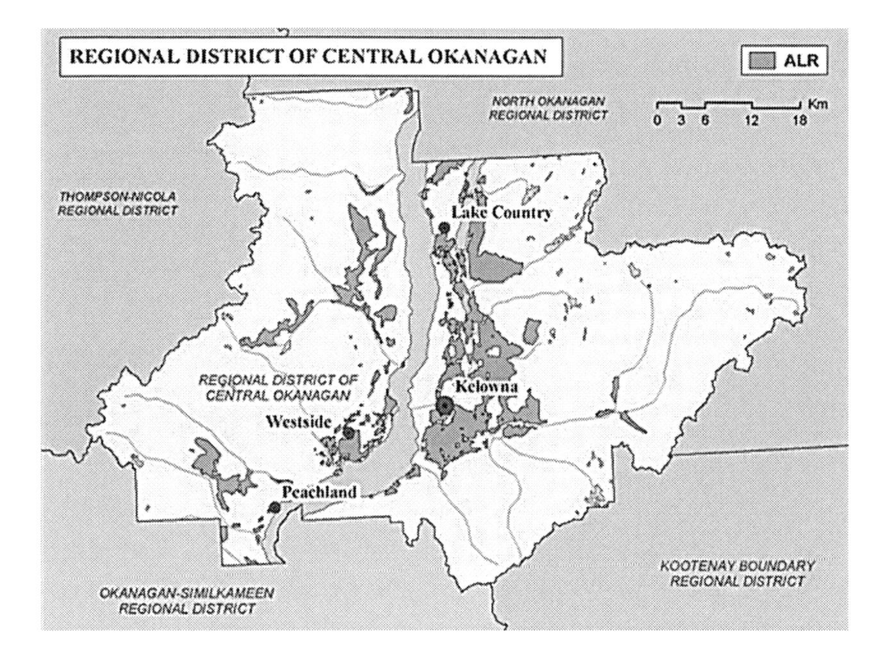

Figure 1. shows a map of the RDCO with the lands classified as ALR highlighted in dark grey.

Why the ALR was created in the first place, and why is there an ongoing controversy after 44 years of enforcement? To answer the first question, BC is not blessed with an abundance of land suitable for agricultural production even though it is the 3rd largest province in Canada. Prime farm land existed in the river valleys where towns also began to support the local farmers and ranchers. As the towns grew into cities, more and more of this prime land was taken out of production. In the late 1960's and early 1970's, nearly 6,000 hectares of prime agricultural land were being lost each year to urban sprawl and other uses. In order to save the scarce arable land for future generations, the provincial government passed the Land Commission Act.

Regarding why there is still some controversy, some land owners are still opposed philosophically to having the use of their land legislated. Other landowners may have bought ALR property with the expectation of the property being eventually released from the ALR, but no such luck. No doubt there are many residential property owners wishing adjacent farm land would be released from the ALR so they would not have to put up with the sights, sounds and smells of food production.

Between 1974 and 1976, 4.7 million hectares (11.6 million acres) were placed in the ALR, approximately 5% of the province land base. Only half of ALR-zoned land is suitable for a range of crops.

In 1996 the provincial government enacted the *Farm Practices Protection Act* (FPPA/ Right-to-Farm), and a number of additional legislative initiatives in support of agriculture. The FPPA basically protects farm operations which follow 'normal farm practices' from complaints, injunctions or court orders related to any nuisance (e.g. odours, noise, dust) created as a result of farm operations. Agricultural operations not in the ALR are not protected by this legislation.

If you are thinking of purchasing property next to ALR land, you should be aware of what the land could be used for if it is not currently in production. Alternatively, if you are seeking to live next to an open space or farm to escape close neighbours, check to see if the land is in the ALR. If it is not, it could soon be developed for any number of purposes other than agricultural. At least if it is ALR land, you will know what to expect based on the table of permitted uses below.

Anyone thinking of purchasing ALR land to generate income should also be aware of what uses are permitted before you go to a lot of time and expense making plans for the land. The following table of permitted uses is not inclusive of all activities, so check the online Agricultural Land Reserve, Permitted Use, Subdivision and Procedure regulations for more details. Also check with the RDCO and the City of Kelowna for any local restrictions or prohibitions.

The City of Kelowna has recently adopted a revised Agriculture Plan, a strategy and framework document developed to facilitate the collaboration of the City and the local agriculture sector to work towards these goals:

- Develop clear policies that serve to protect and promote agriculture;
- Identify opportunities to strengthen farming as an economic driver;
- Increase the amount of, and access to, locally grown and produced food;
- Promote and celebrate the agricultural character of Kelowna; and
- Build resilience in communities against rising costs of food and risks from climate change.

Common farming and ranching activities.	Food and forage crop production, dairy, intensive livestock and poultry operations, greenhouses, nurseries, mushrooms, vineyards, and bee keeping.
Farm uses linked to agriculture (can be restricted but not prohibited by local government).	Wineries & cideries, farm retail sales, storage, packing & processing of farm products, temporary or seasonal agri-tourism activities, timber production, harvesting and silviculture, agroforestry, equestrian facilities.
Farm uses that may or may not be linked directly to agriculture and are considered compatible with agriculture and have low impacts on the land base. Permitted uses can be prohibited by local governments.	Home-based business (including bed and breakfast), temporary sawmill (subject to conditions), conservation and passive recreation and open land parks, pet kennels and breeding facilities, education and research (not schools), agri-tourism accommodation, aggregate extraction less than 500 m3, etc.

Regulatory changes in 1988 resulted in golf courses being classified as a permitted use of agricultural land, which resulted in 181 applications by 1991, covering 8,400 ha of ALR land. Some applications included residential developments and resort hotels. The government removed golf courses as a permitted use in 1992, after allowing only 89 of the 181 applications.

Single landowners, local governments, Treaty First Nation Governments, or their agents can make an application to have land removed from the ALR.

Between April 1, 1974 and March 31, 2016, the land area zoned ALR has decreased by 2.1% but still represents about 5% of BC's total land area. Since 1974 the area of the ALR in Kelowna has decreased 14%. About **40%,** or 8,621 ha (21,302 acres) of Kelowna's current land base (21,235 ha or 52,471 ac) excluding water, Indian reserves, and rights of way is within the ALR. This situation creates an extensive interface between residential developments and agricultural land. You will understand this better once you travel in and around the city.

The increasing pressure to open up more land for development in Kelowna and the RDCO has forced prime ALR land sales prices to reach record highs. The average list price of seven Kelowna properties with orchards and one or more residences listed in November 2017 was $553,563/ha ($224,114/acre). The land available in Kelowna for new developments gets scarcer and scarcer each year, forcing the city to increase residential density and build up rather than out. Most new residential developments are on hillsides and hilltops outside of the ALR. You would think residents would resent the ALR for the impact it is having on development and cost of farmland; however, a May 20, 2015 online poll conducted by Kelowna's Castanet.net showed that 73% of 1,377 respondents said farmland should be protected in the ALR.

So what are the arguments for and against the ALR that can still make the headlines since implementation of the *Land Commission Act* in 1973?

Proponents argue that the ALR:

1. Preserves an essential limited resource for current and future food security and protects a vital industry from development.

2. Forces municipalities to adopt more coordinated or regional land use and transportation strategies to replace sprawl with density.
3. Provides a reasonable extension of the government's right to zone land for various uses in order to protect local farmland for local food production and related uses.

Opponents argue that the ALR:

1. Constitutes unreasonable interference in private property rights.
2. Has inflated property values and created a severe housing shortage throughout British Columbia as a result of this regressive land use policy.
3. Has resulted in many ALR property owners, especially those closer to urban areas where real estate prices are high, to keep their land vacant in anticipation of zoning changes. This is because the ALR does not stipulate that the land must be actively farmed.

In closing, it seems clear that no matter which side of this argument one takes, most residents would agree that if not for the ALR, we would have fewer orchards, vineyards, and market gardens to beautify our city and surrounding country. Additionally, we would have less employment and business generated by agricultural inputs and outputs.

CHAPTER 6

OKANAGAN LAKE

There is no doubt that Okanagan Lake is one of the biggest attractions for tourists and potential newcomers to the area. This amazing body of fresh water provides a playground for numerous fun and exciting activities during many months of the year. Even if one never dips a toe in the water, this fish-filled lake provides a backdrop for breathtaking views as home buyers jostle for properties providing even a peek of this pristine work of Mother Nature.

Let's look at a number of the more interesting facts about Okanagan Lake as provided by various governmental agencies.

1. ***Size:*** The maximum width is 5 km (3.1 mi.) and the maximum length is 135 km (84 mi.) with a total surface area of approximately 351 sq. km (136 sq. mi.). It takes 60 years for all the water in the lake to be flushed out, commonly known as the water residence time of a lake. It is the 8th largest lake in BC, however it doesn't quite make the list of the top 50 largest lakes in Canada.

2. ***Depth:*** The average depth is 76 m (249 ft.) and the deepest portion is 232 m (761 ft.). According to Lakelubbers.com, Okanagan Lake is the 6th deepest lake in BC and the 15th deepest in all of Canada, just behind Lake Ontario.

3. ***Temperature:*** Okanagan Lake reaches lows of about 1° - 3°C (34° - 37°F) during winter months and highs of about 22°C (72°F) in mid-August. For comparison, the Canadian Red

Cross recommends that the most healthful swimming pool temperature is 25.5° - 27.8°C (78° - 82°F).

While we can find no consensus, our research has shown that Okanagan Lake has frozen over only three times in the last century (1906 / 1929 / 1949). In fact, it is even rare for ice to form along the shore.

4. ***Swimming:*** Okanagan Lake is a very enjoyable lake for swimming. The main beaches are tested regularly for contaminants and a swimming advisory warning will be posted on any beaches showing results potentially hazardous to swimmers.

5. ***Can You Drink The Water?*** Depending upon the time of year and the location, Okanagan Lake can look crystal clear and tempting to sip on a hot day. While a mouthful taken while plunging off ones water skis won't kill you, untreated lake water is not potable. The City of Kelowna draws water from the lake and purifies it for users of its water system.

6. ***William R. Bennett Bridge:*** Named after former BC Premier Bill Bennett, this engineering marvel replaced the original "floating" bridge and was completed in 2008. It is 1060 m (3478 ft.) long and is supported by nine concrete pontoons. The navigation span on the west side of the bridge is 44 m (144 ft.) long and provides 18 m (59 ft.) of clearance for vessels to pass under.

   Three lanes are for westbound traffic and two lanes are for eastbound traffic.

   There is a 1.3 m (4 ft. 3 in.) wide pedestrian and cyclist pathway on the south (eastbound) side of the bridge.

7. ***Boat Launches:*** There are five public boat launches within the city limits.

   - Queensway – 238 Queensway Avenue
   - Water Street – 1354 Water Street

- Sutherland Park – 700 Ellis Street
- Cook Road (beside the Eldorado Hotel) – 500 Cook Road
- Cedar Creek Park – 5200 Lakeshore Road. The City of Kelowna advises that this launch site is only suitable for launching small boats and parking is extremely limited.

8. ***Beaches:*** Kelowna has nine swimming beaches within our city limits and each are described in Chapter 20.
9. ***Fish Stocks:*** A 2005 report done in part by the BC Ministry of Water Land and Air Protection states that there are twenty-one fish species in Okanagan Lake. Further information on this subject is presented in Chapter 29.

Boaters are responsible for the wake of their boats and can be held liable for any damage to the shoreline. Boat speed limit is 10 kph (6 mph) within 30 m (100 ft.) of shore.

Kelowna has adopted Ogopogo, a mysterious and much sought lake monster, as a tourist attraction and symbol. It is based on N'ha-a-itk, a supernatural water spirit of the Okanagan First Nations.

As much as the lake provides wonderful recreational activities, it can also wreak havoc when lake levels exceed normal values, as happened in 2017. According to the City of Kelowna Community Trends Report 2017, A Changing Climate, the near record levels of precipitation from March to May, and a rapid snow pack melt, resulted in lake inflows 229% above normal. This led to:

- The second highest lake level ever recorded (343.25 m above sea level; 0.8 m above full pool) closing all beaches for weeks;
- Placement of close to two million sand bags;

- About 3,200 residents affected (including residents living in flood plains);
- Expenditure of at least $12 million for property protection and restoration;
- About 92 of approximately 378 private docks suffered damage or were destroyed;
- High turbidity that forced the City water utility to issue a water quality advisory for the first time in over 21 years; and
- A 7% decrease in hotel occupancy for July 2017 compared to July 2016.

In conclusion, we would like to suggest that every effort be made to ensure our magnificent lake remains healthy and safe, not only for its denizens, but also for the enjoyment of future citizens and visitors.

CHAPTER 7

WEATHER CONDITIONS AND COMPARISONS

When one is thinking of moving to a new city, the topic of weather switches from "small talk" to important business. The business we refer to is the business of "quality of life". The question we will try to answer in this chapter is, "Will my quality of life improve if we move to Kelowna, at least in terms of the impact that weather conditions may have?"

To answer this question, we will present some data on the historical weather patterns for the Kelowna area. In addition, we will present some comparative data so that you can get a feel for how Okanagan weather compares to other cities in North America.

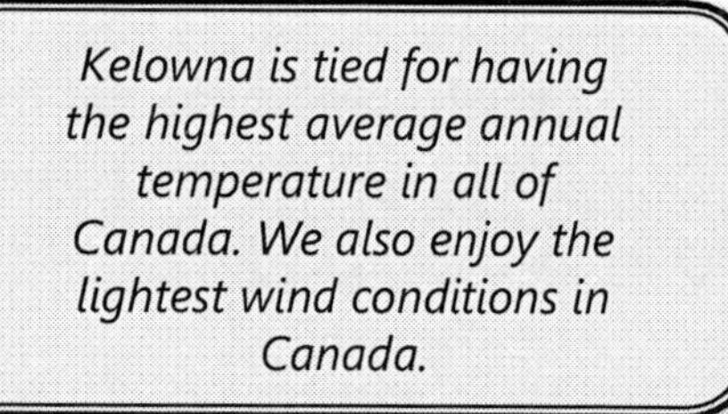

Before we do that, you may find the data points below from the Environment Canada website to be of interest. This data describes the typical weather at the Kelowna International Airport weather station over the course of an average year. It is based on the historical records from 1993 to 2012.

- Kelowna has a continental climate with warm summers and no dry season. The area within 40 km of this station is covered by forests (89%), lakes and rivers (7%), and grasslands (3%).

- Over the course of a year, the temperature typically varies from 6°C (43°F) to 29°C (84°F) and is rarely below -13°C (9°F) or above 34°C (93°F).
- The warm season lasts from June 17 to September 8 with an average daily high temperature about 23°C (73°F). The hottest day of the year is July 30, with an average high of 29°C (84°F) and low of 12° C (54°F).
- The cold season lasts from November 13 to March 3 with an average daily high temperature below 6°C (43°F). The coldest day of the year is December 27, with an average low of -6°C (21°F) and high of 0°C (32°F).
- Out of 72 weather categories, Kelowna ranks best for having the lightest winds year-round at 5.4 km/hr., and for having the most days with light wind (5 km/h or below) at 363!

The warming effects of Okanagan Lake, combined with mountains separating most of BC from the Prairies, moderates the winter climate. However, Arctic air masses do occasionally penetrate the valley during winter, usually for very short periods. The coldest recorded temperature in the city was -36.1 °C (-33.0 °F) recorded on 30 December 1968.

Now, on to what we believe is another enlightening portion of this chapter . . . the comparative data. The average monthly temperatures for nine cities are presented below.

Table 1. Average monthly temperatures (°C) for selected cities in North America and Mexico.

City	J	F	M	A	M	J	J	A	S	O	N	D
Victoria	5	5	7	9	12	15	17	17	14	10	6	4
Vancouver	4	5	7	9	13	16	18	18	15	10	6	4
Kelowna	**-2**	**0**	**4**	**8**	**13**	**17**	**20**	**19**	**14**	**7**	**2**	**-3**

Calgary	-7	-5	-2	5	10	14	16	16	11	5	-2	-7
Regina	-14	-11	-5	5	11	16	19	18	12	4	-5	-12
Winnipeg	-16	-13	-6	4	11	17	20	19	13	5	-5	-13
Toronto	-5	-4	0	7	13	19	22	21	16	10	4	-2
Halifax	-6	-5	-1	4	10	15	19	19	15	9	3	-2
Palm Springs	12	16	18	22	26	30	33	33	30	24	18	14
Puerto Vallarta	25	24	24	25	27	28	29	29	28	29	27	26

Source: Gov't of Canada Canadian Climate Normals 1981-2010 Station Data.

The following highlights reveal how Kelowna ranks among 33 major cities in Canada based on six important criteria. Please note that in most cases data is supplied for all of the 33 cities, however, in some instances data was not available.

- Average Annual Temperature – highest at 15° C (59° F)
  1st / 33 (tied with Abbotsford, Vancouver, and Victoria)

- Average Annual Precipitation – lowest at 345 ml (13.6 in.)
  1st / 33

- Average Afternoon Humidity at 52%
  2nd / 27 (only Calgary has lower humidity)

- Average Annual Snowfall at 63.5 cm (25 in.)
  4th / 33 (only Abbotsford, Vancouver, and Victoria were lower)

- Average Number of Days Without Sun at 61
  10th / 26

- Per Cent of Daylight Hours With Bright Sunshine at 40%
  24th / 26 (tied with Abbotsford and Sherbrook, ON)

Now, you may be wondering . . . how can this be? How can "sunny" Kelowna rank so poorly in these last two categories? The answer to this question in two words is "temperature inversion". Kelowna weather conditions during December and January are the cloudiest in Canada outside of Newfoundland thanks to persistent valley cloud. As Okanagan Lake rarely ever freezes, warmer air rising from the lake climbs above colder atmospheric air creating a temperature inversion which can cause the valley to be socked-in by cloud for weeks on end, with no respite.

So yes, Kelowna is a very "sunny" place to live for most of the year, but the winter months can be a bit of a downer. We discuss more about our cloudy winters and ways to cope with this weather phenomenon in Chapter 39.

We trust that after reading this brief chapter you will be adequately prepared to impress your friends with some fact-filled "small talk" of your own.

See Chapter 40 for our trusted business contact offering a discount on heating and air conditioning services.

CHAPTER 8

HEALTH CARE

Accessibility and quality of health care services are very important factors that families and retirees should consider when moving to a new community. In this chapter we will begin with a description of how health care services are administered and delivered provincially and regionally in BC, and close with a description of the current status of health care facilities and services in Kelowna.

Under the *Medicare Protection Act,* all eligible residents of BC must enroll in the Medical Services Plan of BC (MSP) which insures medically-required services provided by physicians and supplementary health care practitioners, and diagnostic procedures. New residents or persons re-establishing residence are eligible for benefits after a wait period, including the balance of the month of arrival in BC plus two months. New or returning residents arriving from outside Canada should contact a private insurance company for coverage during this period. Further details about eligibility are available on the MSP website.

BC is the only province in which residents pay a monthly health care premium. Effective January 1, 2018, the premiums were cut by 50% for all residents. Individuals and families with an adjusted annual net income of less than $24,000 do not pay any premium, and those earning up to $42,000 adjusted net income may qualify for Premium Assistance. The maximum monthly premiums for individuals and families earning more than $42,000 adjusted annual net income are $75.00 and $150.00, respectively.

Eligible residents can enroll in BC PharmaCare which helps BC residents with the cost of eligible prescription drugs, and certain medical supplies and pharmacy services.

BC implemented PharmaNet to increase patient safety from certain risks associated with the prescribing of drugs. It is a province-wide network that links all BC pharmacies to a central set of data systems. Using PharmaNet, pharmacists can quickly identify — and warn you about — potentially harmful medication interactions. Your PharmaNet information is also available to hospital emergency departments and some community health practices, hospitals and mental health facilities..

Since 1995, PharmaCare coverage of drugs is based on the Reference Drug Program which encourages cost-effective prescribing for common medical conditions. The RDP lists eight categories of drugs that treat the same illness or medical condition with equal effectiveness. You may want to check the online list of eligible drugs under the RDP if you are currently or soon to be purchasing prescribed drugs for an existing medical condition.

To oversee the co-ordination and delivery of provincial programs and highly specialized health care services, the government created the Provincial Health Services Authority. This authority works with the province's other four health authorities and the Ministry of Health to deliver health care services at the local level. Kelowna falls within the Interior Health Authority. In late 2016, Interior Health Authority (IHA) moved into a new office building in downtown Kelowna which consolidated its various offices/service outlets from around the city.

Now we'll turn to the current status of health care services in Kelowna. Demand for services due to a rapidly increasing and aging population over the last 25 years prompted the Kelowna General Hospital (KGH) to undertake a major expansion to upgrade and modernize various facilities such as the:

- Central Okanagan Hospice House (24-bed hospice palliative care facility)

- Sindi Ahluwalia Hawkins Centre (cancer treatment centre)
- Academic Campus Building (affiliated with the university of BC Okanagan, Faculty of Medicine)
- Centennial Patient Care Tower with new rooftop helipad and emergency department
- East Pandosy Clinical Support Building
- Interior Heart and Surgical Centre
- Cardiac Cath Laboratory completed in 2017

The Kelowna General Hospital is home to 600 physicians with hospital privileges,400 beds and nearly 800 volunteers.

Today the KGH offers about 120 high-level, specialty medical care services including 24-hour emergency and trauma services, ambulatory and outpatient clinics, and diagnostic/paramedical services. Surgeons can now perform up to 600 open-heart operations annually at the KGH. This hospital also serves as the referral hospital for close to 750,000 people living in the Southern Interior.

The Kelowna General Hospital (KGH) Foundation is raising $8 million to support construction of JoAnna's House between fall 2018 and fall 2019. This 20-room residence will provide a home-away-from-home for families traveling to the KGH for care. The KGH Foundation, in collaboration with the Canadian Mental Health Association (CMHA), raised the funds necessary to open Foundry Kelowna in September 2017. This facility provides a one-stop-shop for young people to voluntarily access mental health care, substance use services, primary care, social services and youth and family peer supports. The CMHA plans to also operate a mobile Foundry beginning in summer 2018 to deliver services throughout the Kelowna CMA.

Unfortunately with the expansion of the hospital facilities, services and patient and visitor traffic, staff and visitor parking has become a major issue, even with the addition of a parkade and parking lots. We strongly suggest you download a copy of the KGH Parking and Access map from the KGH website and have it handy to consult before you plan a hospital or emergency department visit. As an example of the patient traffic, 75,951 people visited the department in 2015/16, along with 24,428 patients undergoing one-day out-patient services.

Kelowna residents can face long wait times to see specialists and for certain surgical procedures much like other cities in Canada. You can check the BC government website Surgery Wait Times for information about wait times for elective surgical procedures in British Columbia.

Newcomers to Kelowna and area have reported difficulty finding a family doctor after arriving. According to the College of Physicians and Surgeons of BC, there were 259 family physicians practicing in the Kelowna CMA in January 2018 (1.33/1000 population).

Figure 1 shows the number of General Practitioners/Family Physicians per 1000 population in some major Census Metropolitan Areas across Canada in 2015. The Kelowna CMA was just below the average (1.34) of the selected 14 CMAs.

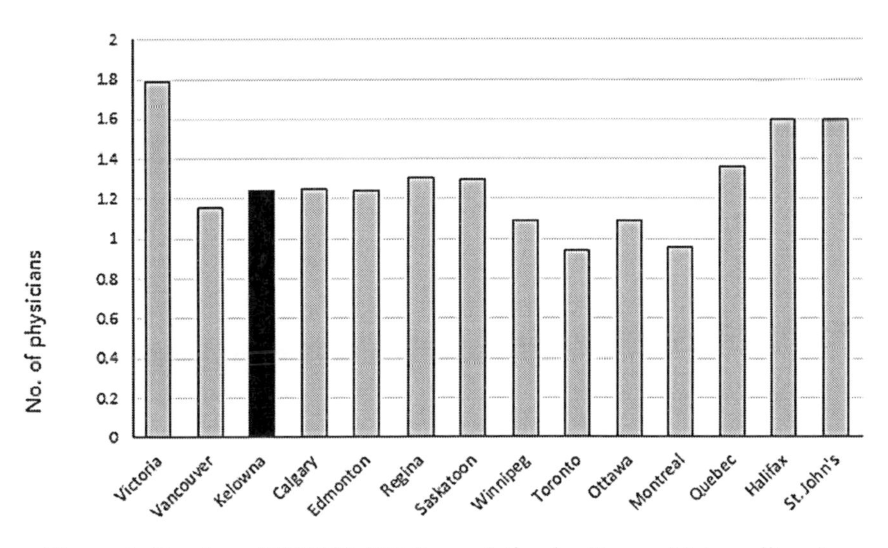

Figure 1. Number of GP/FP's/1000 population by Census Metropolitan Area (CMA), 2015.

Source: Physicians, Canadian Medical Associations; populations, StatsCan.

In order to avoid disappointment, you should start your search for a family doctor before you arrive. Consider getting a referral from your current family doctor, or contacting friends or family in Kelowna to suggest some doctors. There are no guarantees of success, but it never hurts to ask.

A search of the College of Physicians and Surgeons of BC's *Find a Physician* web page in January 2018 revealed only one family physician taking new patients in the Kelowna CMA. Statistics Canada reported that 85.5% of 138,860 residents in the metropolitan Kelowna area had a regular medical doctor in 2013 and 2014.

The first class of thirty medical doctors using the Academic Campus Building graduated in 2015 which will hopefully increase the number of family physicians in Kelowna and area.

Most people would prefer to remain in their homes rather than in a health care facility, if at all possible. To this end there are several at-home and community services available in Kelowna to support people with acute, chronic, palliative or rehabilitative health care needs. You can obtain useful information on such services from Interior Health Authority's (IHA) online publication *Guide to Home and Community Care.*

In July 2017, Interior Health created two mobile safe injection sites for illicit drug users where supervision is available on a voluntary basis. Trained health workers are available to provide advice and materials on addictions harm reduction and treatment options.

In summary, Kelowna residents have the same access to first-class medical and non-medical health services as one would expect in larger urban centres. Interior Health's mission is to: *"promote healthy lifestyles and provide needed health services in a timely, caring, and efficient manner, to the highest professional and quality standards."* We can only hope that Interior Health receives sufficient funding to accomplish its mission.

CHAPTER 9

CHILD CARE

One of the most important aspects of moving to a new city, especially for working parents, is that of finding quality and affordable care for one's pre-school children. Another question is that of availability. We will try to shine some light on each of these areas so that new families are as well-prepared as they can be before they join us.

1. Where Are They?

One great source of information for newcomers with children is the Kelowna Child Care Society (KCCS) which provides a list of licensed, and registered not licensed, child care providers in Kelowna. Their referral service is funded by the BC government, and at the time of writing, their site listed 109 service providers within Kelowna, for children ranging from 30 months to school-age. Another informative site is the BC Child Care Map which lists over 100 care providers in the Kelowna area. The cool thing about this site is that you can easily see where child care providers are located in relation to where you may be looking to find a home.

2. Quality Levels

Even some young local families have a difficult time determining which service providers might provide the best care for their children. Now, imagine the challenge for newcomers who may have few, if any, friends or family to rely on for referrals. Handing your children over to strangers can be a traumatic experience for many parents. Below are some tips on determining which caregivers offer high-quality services. We have learned this from our own family members and from our online research.

- Interior Health Inspection reports – You can go online to determine if the licensed service provider that you are considering has infractions registered against their facility.
- Personal visits – It goes without saying that showing up unannounced to see how a facility is run may be one of the best actions to take.
- Check online reviews – This is an area that is beginning to develop and provide much-needed insight for existing and new parents. Try godaycare.com which we know offers free review information, although it was limited to only a few reviews for the Kelowna area at the time of writing. Another free service is daycarereviews.ca
- Call the Kelowna Child Care Society – We aren't sure if they will give opinions on their membership however they should be able to assist you in other ways.

3. Cost

The reality is that for the majority of parents, the cost of child care is becoming almost as important as the quality aspect.

Our goal is to give potential newcomers a relative idea of how child care costs compare to their former place of residence. This comparison can be very complex in that each province has varying taxation levels, subsidy programs, and fee caps which are beyond the scope of this publication.

An often quoted study on child care costs in Canada is titled, *A Growing Concern - 2016 Child Care Fees in Canada's Big Cities,* produced by the Canadian Centre for Policy Alternatives. Table 1 shows data on the comparative median monthly child care fees reported in the document.

Unfortunately, Kelowna was not included in this study and therefore we used an estimate of costs from The Kelowna Child Care Society 2016 Survey and included it in this table for ease of comparison. It is also important to point out the enigma of the Quebec cities, where the province has capped daycare costs at $7.30 a day per child. Lastly, all jurisdictions except Quebec use parent fee subsidies.

Table 1. Comparative median monthly child care fees – 2016.

City	Monthly Fee*		
	Infant	Toddler	Preschool
Vancouver	1,360	1,292	950
Kelowna (est.)	**758**	**750**	**750**
Calgary	1,102	1,050	1,000
Edmonton	990	891	885
Regina	875	635	575
Winnipeg	651	451	451
Hamilton	1,062	1,052	931
Toronto	1.758	1,354	1,212
Montreal	168	168	168
St. John	868	716	694
Halifax	910	825	823

*Includes both centre & home care locations. Source: Canadian Centre for Policy Alternatives.

The Kelowna Child Care Society has prepared an annual survey of its service-providing members since 2007. The most recent survey is from 2016 and revealed the following costs:

2016 Median Monthly Fee - Kelowna			
Infant	$758	Range	$625 - $1000
Toddler	$750	Range	$625 - $900
Pre-School	$750	Range	$625 - $900

The second source of child care cost information is from godaycare.com. From what we can tell, this is a relatively new site and their data appears to be derived from Central Canadian locations. We mention it here because the site may contain particular information of value to readers which is often difficult to obtain. Below is a synopsis of their posted cost data which is relevant for comparative purposes.

BC Average Monthly Fee (Licensed)			
Infant	$969	No. of Respondents	1,939
Toddler	$869	No. of Respondents	1,724
Pre-School	$760	No. of Respondents	1,090

Canadian Average Monthly Fee (Licensed)			
Infant	$944	No. of Respondents	12,671
Toddler	$830	No. of Respondents	8,979
Pre-School	$766	No. of Respondents	5,034

4. Child Care Subsidies in British Columbia

For those newcomers arriving from outside of BC, we would be remiss if we didn't discuss child care subsidies. A child care subsidy, or allowance, is available to help low income families in BC with the cost of child care:

- Families earning $40,000 or less should apply – families earning up to $55,000 may also be eligible;
- Families may be eligible for full or partial subsidy, depending on their circumstances and income.

Eligible child care arrangements must be one of the following:

- Licensed family home, group child care centre or preschool;
- Registered 'license-not-required' home;
- License-not-required home or in the child's own home.

Parents or guardians must also meet one or more of the following criteria:

- You are employed or self-employed;
- You are attending an educational institution or enrolled in distance education;
- You are seeking employment or participating in an employment-related program (only one parent can be looking for work);
- You have a medical condition that interferes with your ability to care for your child;
- You have a child attending a licensed preschool;
- You have been referred by a social worker from the Ministry of Children and Family Development or a delegated Aboriginal agency.

The child care subsidy is paid directly to the child care provider (except in the case of care in the child's home), and the parent is responsible for paying the difference between the full cost of care and the amount that the subsidy covers. Further details about the child care subsidy program are available on the BC Government Child Care Subsidy website.

While we were unable to find the average subsidy amount for each child in Kelowna, we were able to determine that the BC average subsidy per child in 2015/2016 was approximately $564/month. This data is from the BC Ministry of Children & Family Development Performance Management report. Thanks to funding from the provincial government, Kelowna will add 132 spaces to its inventory in 2018.

One can draw their own conclusions from the information in this chapter, however it seems safe to say that, subsidies aside, Kelowna has lower child care costs than most large Canadian cities.

CHAPTER 10

EDUCATION

Although debatable, education is probably the topic most important to many newcomers. The first section of this chapter will benefit families with children; the balance of the chapter focuses on adult education.

Primary, Middle, and Secondary Education

The primary, middle, and secondary school system is administered by the Central Okanagan School District #23 which includes a few schools outside the Kelowna area. Given that the curriculum is managed by this central organization, and the fact that kids from different municipalities interact together, especially in extra-curricular activities, it seems appropriate to cover this topic according to the district boundaries.

A complete list of all schools in the Central Okanagan School District #23 is available at www.sd23.bc.ca. Below are a few key data points taken from this site.

- The district area includes approximately 198,300 citizens living in 4 municipalities - Peachland, West Kelowna, Kelowna, Lake Country, and the Regional District of Central Okanagan.
- It serves about 22,000 students and is the 5th largest district in BC.
- It includes 43 schools of which 31 are elementary, 6 are middle, 5 are secondary and 1 is an alternative school.

Many families with school-aged children will do the same amount of research on the education system as they do on the local job market. Further, many newcomers often determine where they will buy or rent their home, based on how they feel about the schools in the area.

The challenge is how does one evaluate the quality of the education system right down to the school level? Many will rely on the opinions of friends already living in the school district. Others may interview district administrators, school teachers or principals to try to get a feel of how things might be run in a particular school.

Another option for parents is to research school ratings. Now this is one very controversial method, nonetheless it certainly warrants investigation. We are referring to the school rankings done by the Fraser Institute. Below is an excerpt from their website:

> *The Fraser Institute is an independent, non-partisan research and educational organization based in Canada. Our research is peer-reviewed and overseen by an Editorial Advisory Board of leading international scholars. The Fraser Institute promotes transparency in research – in other words, our methodology is open and clearly explained, and others can replicate our conclusions. In addition, the source of our data is always provided.*

Table 1 shows how the Fraser Institute ranked our District high schools for 2015-16. These were the latest results available prior to publication.

Table 1. Local and provincial ranking of Kelowna-area high schools, 2015-16.

Local Ranking	Provincial Ranking (/293)	Secondary School
1	25	Okanagan Mission
2	28	Aberdeen Hall Senior
3	30	Kelowna Christian
4	67	Heritage Christian
5	71	Kelowna Secondary

6a	120	Immaculata Catholic
6b	120	George Elliot
7	173	Mount Boucherie
8	193	Rutland Senior

Notes: Schools numbered 2; 3; 4; and 6a are independent secondary schools. Kelowna Secondary is the only French immersion school. Source: Fraser Institute.

The Fraser Institute did not rank our middle schools (grades 6-9) as they do not meet all of their criteria for ranking. Most of our elementary schools were ranked for 2015/2016 as shown in the next table.

Table 2. Local and provincial ranking of Kelowna-area elementary schools, 2015-2016.

Local Ranking	Provincial Ranking (/956)	School
1	41	Aberdeen Hall
2	131	Kelowna Christian
3	163	St Joseph
4	300	Anne McClymont
5	368	Casorso
6	388	Chute Lake
7	496	Glenmore
8	518	Quigley
9	548	North Glenmore
10	569	Black Mountain
11	614	Heritage Christian
12	614	Bankhead
13	663	Dorothea Walker
14	663	Watson Road
15	695	South Kelowna
16	721	Ellison
17	738	A S Matheson
18	738	Pearson Road
19	771	Belgo
20	781	Raymer
21	816	Rose Valley
22	828	Rutland
23	828	Spring Valley

24	841	Hudson Road
25	916	South Rutland

Notes: Schools numbered 1, 2 3, and 11 are independent. Schools numbered 5, 9, 13, and 19 are K-6 French immersion. Total number of elementary schools ranked was 956.

Post-Secondary Education

Kelowna is very fortunate to be home to a number of quality post-secondary educational institutions.

1. University of British Columbia – Okanagan Campus (UBCO)

According to the UBCO fact sheet, published in April of 2016, there were over 8,300 funded spaces for the 2017/2018 academic year. It further states that:

> *The University of British Columbia is the third largest university in Canada. UBC is a global centre of research and learning with state-of-the-art facilities on campuses in Point Grey and downtown Vancouver, as well as UBC Okanagan in Kelowna.*
>
> *UBC Okanagan offers undergraduate and graduate programs in a range of disciplines.*
>
> *Undergraduate programs include applied science, arts, education, fine arts, health studies, health and social development, management, and science.*
>
> *Graduate programs include biology, chemistry, education, engineering, English, environmental sciences, fine arts, interdisciplinary graduate studies, management, mathematics, nursing, psychology and social work.*

In 2017, the Times Higher Education ranked UBCO the most international university in North America for the fourth consecutive year. The UBCO website includes an impressive amount of information for students. Table 3 contains a few of their facts and figures for 2017.

Table 3. Facts and figures about UBCO, 2017.

Student Population	8,718 (7,930 undergraduate and 788 graduates)
Faculty Population	518 faculty
Staff Population	652 staff and 951 student employees
Faculties and Schools	8 (Including the Faculty of Medicine's Southern Medical Program)
Campus Housing	1,676 total beds
Size of Campus	209 hectares (516 acres)
Buildings area	135,498 sq. m (about 1.5 mil. sq. ft.)
Annual Research Funding	$14.5 million from more than 700 research projects underway

2. Okanagan College (OC)

Okanagan College is a public, post-secondary institution with over 120 certificates, diplomas, degrees and programs including apprenticeship and pre-apprenticeship trades programs. Its largest campus is located in Kelowna. Okanagan College has grown to be the largest college in BC outside the Lower Mainland and Victoria. It is the second-largest trade school in BC. Approximately 430 international students from over thirty countries currently study at Okanagan College.

The College's four main campuses are located in Penticton, Kelowna, Vernon and Salmon Arm. Table 4 lists information about the college.

Table 4. Facts and figures about Okanagan College, 2017.

Student Population (Fall 2017)	8,463
Faculty Population	269
Vocational Instructors	286
Staff Population	1,029
No. of Program Areas (Programs)	12 (184)
Student Housing Beds	143
Size of Kelowna Campus	15.79 hectares (39 acres)
Kelowna Campus Building	49,772 m^2 (535,741 $ft.^2$)
Annual Research Funding	$600k - $900k

Programs of interest to international students include: English as a Second Language (ESL) courses, vocational and trades programs and four-year degrees in both Business (BBA) and Computer Information Systems (BCIS). Many students also choose the university transfer program which allows students a smooth transition and cost-saving entry method into many of Canada's most prestigious universities. The college also has a long history of successful study tours, student exchanges and customized group training programs.

3. Private Training Institutions

The Private Training Institutions Branch (PTIB) of the BC Ministry of Advanced Education administers the Private Training Act and associated regulations. Table 5 lists the private training institutions and their certificate type in the Kelowna area.

Table 5. Private training institutions located in Kelowna and type of certificates granted.

Institution	Certificate Type
Academy of Learning College	Designated[1]
Canadian School of Natural Nutrition	Registered[2]
Canscribe Career College	Designated
Career City College	Registered
Centre for Arts and Technology	Designated
Diving Dynamics	Designated
First College	Registered
Focus College of Professionals Ltd.	Designated
Interior Heavy Equipment Operator School Ltd.	Designated
Kelowna College of Professional Counselling	Designated
Lighthouse Labs	Designated
M.C. College	Designated
Okanagan Mountain Helicopters FTU Ltd.	Designated
SICA Construction Training Centre	Designated
Southern Interior Flight Centre	Registered

Sprott Shaw College	Designated
Studio Chi	Registered
Taylor Pro Training Ltd.	Designated
Vancouver Career College	Designated
VanWest College (Kelowna)	Designated

[1]Designation is associated with a higher level of quality. Only designated institutions can apply for the BC Education Quality Assurance (EQA) designation and, once EQA is achieved, enroll international students on study permits, and apply for StudentAidBC (SABC).
[2]Registration is the minimum requirement for private training institutions offering career-related programs with 40 or more hours of instruction, and for which tuition is at least $4,000.

4. Theological Institutions

There are no theological post-secondary educational institutions in the Central Okanagan.

5. Aboriginal-Controlled Post-Secondary Institutes

The Indigenous Adult and Higher Learning Association reports that there are no Aboriginal controlled post-secondary institutions in the Central Okanagan. Fortunately, the En'owkin Centre in Penticton is only a 40-minute commute. The next closest institution is the Nicola Valley Institute of Technology in Merritt, BC which is approximately a 90-minute commute.

Educational opportunities abound in Kelowna for all ages and aptitudes. We expect this trend will continue to grow as our facilities expand to accommodate growth and the demand for new programs.

CHAPTER 11

OUR AIRPORT KEEPS GROWING AND GROWING . . .

One of the major factors individuals, families and businesses consider when deciding to relocate to another city is airline connections. In today's ever-increasing global movement of people, goods and services, timely and connected air services are essential for any city to attract newcomers, tourists and businesses.

The Kelowna Airport (YLW) is about a 20-minute drive from downtown if Hwy 97 is not too busy. It is served by taxis and public transit buses. Car rental pick-up and drop-off is available from four national companies. There are over 2,600 short- and long-term security-patrolled parking stalls and it always appears to be very full. A valet service also operates year-round if you want your car ready and warm. This service costs $15.00, in addition to the parking fee: short-term rates of $1.50/hour, maximum rates of $18.50/24 hours, and long-term maximum rate of $12.00/24 hours or $62.00/week.

In 2017, Kelowna was the 11th busiest airport by passenger traffic (Table 1). This is not bad for a city that ranked 19th out of the largest metropolitan areas in Canada, based on the 2016 census. In 2017, 1,802,470 passengers used the airport, a new record. Passenger traffic set records every month of 2017 ranging from 2 to 22%. At the time of writing there were up to 60 daily non-stop commercial flights to 15 destinations.

Table 1. Ranking of Canada's busiest airports based on passenger traffic in 2017.

Rank	Airport	No. Passengers (million)
1	Toronto (Pearson)	47.13
2	Vancouver	24.17
3	Montreal	18.16
4	Calgary	16.27
5	Edmonton	7.80
6	Ottawa	4.84
7	Winnipeg	4.31
8	Halifax	4.08
9	Toronto (Billy Bishop)	2.80
10	Victoria	1.93
11	**Kelowna**	**1.89**
12	Quebec City	1.67
13	St. John's	1.53
14	Saskatoon	1.46
15	Regina	1.22

Source: Data compiled from figures reported by listed airports.

Kelowna residents are connected by air to anywhere in the world. YLW is the air hub for the Southern Interior of BC and is made possible by the connections through Calgary, Edmonton, Toronto, Vancouver and Seattle (Table 2). According to Tourism Kelowna, 26% of tourists arrived in Kelowna by air in 2016, due in part to the airport's non-stop and connected airline networks.

Table 2. Airlines serving Kelowna International Airport.

Airlines	Destinations	
	Year Round	Winter
Air Canada	Vancouver, Calgary, Toronto	
Air North	Vancouver, Whitehorse	
Air Transit		Cancun, Puerto Vallarta
Alaska/Horizon Air	Seattle/Tacoma	

Central Mountain Air	Prince George	
Flair Airlines	Edmonton, Vancouver	
Pacific Coastal Airlines	Cranbrook, Victoria	
Sunwing Airlines		Cancun, Varadero
WestJet	Calgary, Edmonton, Toronto, Vancouver, Victoria, Winnipeg	Cancun, Puerto Vallarta, Cabo San Lucas

Source: Kelowna International Airport.

Many people escape the not-so-cold, but somewhat overcast winters using direct flights to Phoenix and popular destinations in Mexico. In addition, Kelowna airport is currently seeking a carrier to connect Kelowna directly with London or Frankfurt.

In March 2016, YLW announced plans to renovate the departure lounge (new fresh food and beverage options), and to build a privately-funded Airport Plaza across from the airport, an outbound baggage hall, a non-passenger vehicle screening facility, and a new commercial development (completion by 2018).

In July 2016, YLW implemented a first-of-its-kind in Canada Farm to Flight program whereby passengers can purchase various local in-season fruits in YLW's departures lounge gift shop. This program is only available for travelers in Canada due to international regulations.

Passengers can also purchase duty free gifts and enjoy full restaurant services outside and inside the departure lounge. In addition, passengers flying within Canada can purchase up to 12 bottles of some of the finest Okanagan wines as carry-on. Staff in the Okanagan Estate Wine Cellar will pack your wine for you in easy-to-carry boxes at no additional charge. Various wineries also offer wine tasting at the airport.

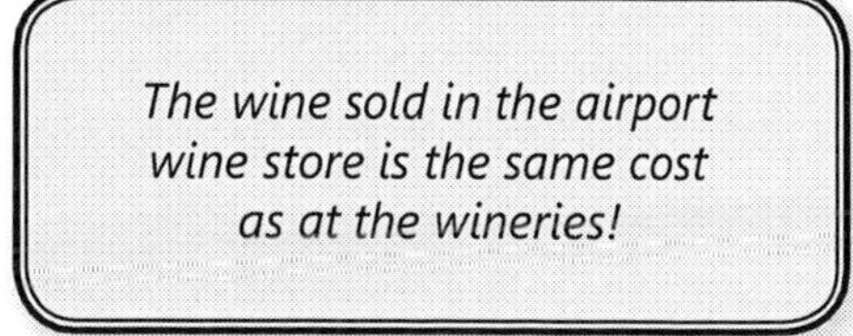

The airport provides many other useful services such as:

- Free baggage carts;
- Board room equipped with audio video equipment;
- Business centre that features private work stations with internet accessible payphones;
- Credit card phones with plug-in internet access for laptop computers;
- Text telephone/teletype centre;
- Relieving area for pets;
- Four electric car chargers.

In November 2016, the airport announced a $259 million expansion plan out to 2045 that will include:

- Extending both ends of terminal;
- Reconfiguring and enlarging international arrivals area;
- Enlarging departure lounge;
- Building new domestic baggage claims area;
- Expanding customs & immigration area;
- Enlarging pre-boarding screening area;
- Upgrading existing runway, taxiway and apron lighting and signage.

The continued growth in passenger traffic has prompted the major airlines to increase the frequency of flights to some of their major destinations in 2018.

In summary, YLW offers the same services as larger international airports, albeit on a somewhat smaller scale, and there is no limit to the destinations you can fly to for business or pleasure.

CHAPTER 12

COST OF LIVING

Undoubtedly, the cost of living can have a significant impact on the quality of life for newcomers. The degree of this impact is what we will address in this chapter, and we trust that it will help you decide if you can comfortably afford to live in Kelowna.

You may have heard of the "Sunshine Tax" that people sometimes refer to in describing what they believe is the high cost of living in the Okanagan. Does this tax really exist? . . . and we are not talking about the 7% Provincial Sales Tax, on top of the 5% Federal Goods & Services Tax. We will let you be the judge as we put the cost of living in Kelowna into context with the rest of Canada.

Before we get started though, you should first know that:

- BC persons earning $122,000 paid the second lowest amount of provincial income tax in 2017 (8.6%);
- BC's general corporate tax rate of 12% is among the lowest in Canada; and
- BC's combined federal-provincial tax rate of 27% is among the lowest of the G7 nations.

Consumer Price Index (CPI)

A useful measurement familiar to most people is the Consumer Price Index (CPI). The federal government uses the CPI as an indicator of the change in the general level of consumer prices or the rate of inflation (annual change). It is obtained by comparing, over time, the cost of a fixed basket of goods and services purchased by consumers. Since the basket contains goods and services of unchanging or equivalent quantity and quality, the index reflects only pure price change. You can compare movements in the CPI to changes in your personal buying power and make necessary adjustments to your family and business budgets.

Table 1 shows Statistic Canada's comparative CPI for all items for December 2017 and the % change (= annual inflation rate) over the previous 12 months

Table 1. December 2017 consumer price indexes and 2017 inflation rates (%).

	Consumer Price Index	% Change (Inflation Rate)
Canada	130.8	1.9
British Columbia	**125.0**	**2.1**
Alberta	137.3	1.6
Saskatchewan	134.4	1.7
Manitoba	130.5	1.6
Ontario	131.9	1.7
Quebec	126.9	1.0
New Brunswick	131.2	2.3
Nova Scotia	132.4	1.1
Prince Edward Island	133.2	1.8
Newfoundland & Labrador	135.7	2.4
Whitehorse	128.8	2.1
Yellowknife	135.1	2.4
Iqualuit	126.0	1.8

Source: Statistics Canada, CANSIM, table 326-0020 and Catalogue nos. 62-001-X and 62-010-X. (Reported Jan. 28, 2018)

As you can see, BC had the lowest CPI of all jurisdictions in 2017, however its position (tied for 4th highest) was not as favourable when the annual rate of inflation was calculated.

Cost of Living Index (CLI)

Two websites, Expatistan.com and Numbeo.com collect prices of goods, services, rents, etc. from posted and published databases and crowdsourcing to calculate and compare cost of living indexes (CLI) among cities around the world. We collected the posted January 2018 CLIs for Canadian cities and calculated the % difference from the posted CLI for Kelowna (Table 2).

Table 2. Percent difference between the CLIs of selected Canadian cities and Kelowna (CLI = 0) based on CLI calculations (January, 2018).

Website	Victoria	Vancouver	**Kelowna**	Calgary	Edmonton	Regina	Winnipeg	Toronto	Ottawa	Montreal	Quebec	Halifax	St. John's
EXP[1]	8	27	**0**	17	11	4	3	24	13	1	-3	1	6
NUM[2]	5	15	**0**	0	0	-7	-12	11	-6	12	21	3	-3

[1] EXP - Expatistan.com
[2] NUM - Numbeo.com (Figures include consumer prices plus monthly rent for 1 and 3 bedroom apartments)

The CLI data from both websites revealed Kelowna had a lower cost of living index than many major Canadian cities. This is not to say that Kelowna comes out cheapest in every category included in the CLI calculations. Far from it! You will read in the next chapter on real estate that Kelowna has higher than average home prices. In addition, you will discover that in October 2017, Kelowna had one of the lowest vacancy rates (0.2%) in Canada, putting upward pressure on rental rates. This data reveals how housing costs could make Kelowna unaffordable for some.

Vehicle Costs

Table 3 reveals how gasoline prices are higher in Kelowna than most cities as of February 8, 2018. Of course, gas prices are very volatile and therefore Table 3 is just a snapshot of the comparative costs at the time of writing. The high price in Kelowna relative to other BC Interior communities, coupled with no price differences among local gasoline retailers, prompt many citizens to cry foul with every price increase. Also, you have to wonder why Kelowna pays more at the pump than Ottawa and Toronto when BC borders a major world petroleum producer.

Table 3. Lowest price of regular gasoline ($/L) for major Canadian cities.

Victoria	Vancouver	**Kelowna**	Calgary	Regina	Winnipeg	Toronto	Ottawa	Montreal	Halifax	St. John's
1.27	1.31	**1.23**	1.03	0.97	0.99	1.15	1.09	1.27	1.15	1.27

Source: GasBuddy.com, February 8, 2018.

Speaking of automobiles, a major cost for many drivers is annual auto insurance premiums. British Columbia, Saskatchewan, Manitoba and Quebec are the only provinces that provide public auto insurance. In BC, all automobile owners must purchase a minimum of **basic** Autoplan Insurance from the Insurance Corporation of BC (ICBC). Drivers have the option of buying **extended** coverage from ICBC, or from a private insurance company. Table 4 shows the results of an analysis of 2015 provincial private auto insurance rates reported by the Ontario Ministry of Finance.

Table 4. Average annual private vehicle insurance premiums by province for 2015.

Province	Premium	Province	Premium
British Columbia	$1,316	Quebec	$724
Alberta	$1,179	New Brunswick	$763

Saskatchewan	$775	Nova Scotia	$783
Manitoba	$1,001	Prince Edward Island	$755
Ontario	$1,458	Newfoundland	$1,090

Source: Deloitte LLP.

The premiums listed in Table 4 have no doubt increased since 2015, the year to which the data applies. Unfortunately, we were unable to find any updated comparative data. In 2015, BC drivers paid the 2nd highest average auto insurance costs among all provinces. ICBC increased basic insurance rates to 6.4% on November 1, 2017, and a similar increase may be approved in late 2018 in order to cover the increasing costs of repair and injury claims due to greatly increased accident rates.

Newcomers have 90 days in which to transfer their driver's license and purchase BC vehicle insurance. If you have driven 4 years claim-free before arrival, or achieve 4 years claim-free after arriving, you qualify for a 43% discount off your ICBC premium. Seniors qualify for a 25 per cent saving on Basic Autoplan if both the vehicle owner and principal operator are 65 or over, and don't use the vehicle for commuting to work, for business use, or for delivery services.

Cost of Accommodations

The single highest monthly expense for most people is housing. Table 5 compares housing affordability in Kelowna to other Canadian cities based on household incomes reported in 2016 for non-farm, non-reserve households. The data excludes households with zero or negative income in 2016. Statistics Canada included the costs of utilities, repairs, maintenance, mortgage cost and property taxes, among other expenses, in its calculations.

The data reveals that Kelowna had the lowest rental vacancy rate in October 2017 (0.2%), the 4th highest percentage of home owners (19.0%) in 2016, and the 2nd highest percentage of renters (46.8%) among all the cities listed that paid more than 30% of their 2016 total income towards shelter costs. Refer to Chapter 14 (Rental Accommodations... or Lack Thereof) for the latest data on renting in Kelowna.

Table 5. Comparative housing ownership, shelter cost and affordability for non-farm, non-reserve private households in selected cities across Canada.

City	% Home owner-ship[1]	Rental va-cancy rate[2]	Average monthly shelter cost ($)[1]		Affordability[1,3]	
			Owner	Renter	Owner	Renter
Victoria	62.6	0.7	1,410	1,117	22.3	48.5
Vancouver	63.7	0.9	1,622	1,242	27.7	41.2
Kelowna	**73.3**	**0.2**	**1,345**	**1,184**	**19.0**	**46.8**
Calgary	73.0	6.3	1,640	1,366	16.5	36.2
Edmonton	69.6	7.0	1,557	1,292	16.4	37.7
Regina	69.9	7.0	1,348	1,161	12.0	46.0
Saskatoon	70.2	9.6	1,408	1,130	14.5	45.1
Winnipeg	67.3	2.8	1,174	940	12.2	39.4
Toronto	66.5	1.1	1,755	1,264	27.3	46.7
Ottawa	66.6	1.7	1,424	1,066	14.1	42.2
Montreal	55.7	2.8	1,263	842	20.1	36.7
Quebec City	60.2	4.5	1,101	796	10.6	31.2
St. John	70.3	4.7	1,031	738	13.8	35.7
Halifax	60.1	2.6	1,268	1,035	12.9	43.1
St. John's	70.0	7.2	1,379	927	14.5	42.7
Canada	67.8	3.0	1,313	1,002	16.5	39.9

Source: [1]Statistics Canada, Census Population, 2016; [2]Canada Mortgage and Housing Corporation, Rental Market Reports, October 2017; [3]% households spending >30% of 2016 total income on shelter costs.

Property Taxes

Another important cost of living expense is the annual property tax collected by municipalities. This tax is based on the assessed value of the land and improvements and the mill rate/$1000 assessed value that is assigned to deliver certain services. Besides the property tax, Kelowna homeowners also pay an annual fee of $174.30 for residential waste collection and a water parcel tax of $50.00. Residents also pay bi-monthly a Flat Rate ($25.07) and a Water Quality Enhancement Fee ($15.77) on top of the graduated cost of water used (the more you use, the more you pay!). Residential property values are adjusted annually, based on sales of similar properties in the area.

Table 6 below presents the estimated 2017 residential and commercial mill rates/$1000 of assessed property value for major cities across Canada. Some residential rates include single family and multi-family residential values. Taxes will vary according to the services provided, location within the municipal boundaries, and any grants or rebates. Kelowna had the second lowest commercial and residential tax rates of all the major cities listed.

Table 6. Comparison of 2017 commercial and residential property tax rates (/$1000) and commercial/residential ratio among selected cities.

City	Commercial	Residential	Ratio
Vancouver	12.44	2.55	4.87
Kelowna	**14.80**	**5.90**	**2.51**
Calgary	17.74	6.50	2.73
Edmonton	20.76	8.51	2.44
Saskatoon	14.57	8.48	1.72
Regina	16.16	9.25	1.75
Winnipeg	24.36	12.15	2.01
Toronto	25.20	6.62	3.81
Ottawa	28.52	10.68	2.67
Montreal	37.23	9.88	3.77
Halifax	33.18	11.98	2.77
St. John's	24.70	7.30	3.38

Source: Data extracted from Altus Group, *Canadian Property Tax Rate Benchmark Report, 2017.*

Eligible home owners in BC can apply for a Home Owner Grant to reduce the amount of residential property taxes that they pay on their primary residence. In 2017, homeowner grants were $770.00 (eligible and under 65) and $1,045.00 (eligible and 65+). Properties must be assessed at less than $1.65 million to be eligible.

Wages and Salaries

We were unable to determine how wages and salaries paid in Kelowna compare to those of other cities. We were, however, able to find comparative provincial/territorial minimum wages and average weekly earnings (Table 7).

Table 7. Provincial/territorial minimum wages and average weekly salaries.

	Minimum Wage		Average Weekly Earnings (Mar. 31, 2017)
	Jan. 1, 2018	Jan. 1, 2019	
National Average	$11.82	$12.11	$1,000.36
British Columbia	**$11.35**	**$12.65**	**$919.25**
Alberta	$13.60	$15.00	$1,118.57
Saskatchewan	$10.96	$11.29[1]	$988.40
Manitoba	$11.15	$11.15	$888.52
Ontario	$14.00	$15.00	$973.56
Quebec	$11.25	$11.25	$878.34
New Brunswick	$11.00	$11.00	$875.15
Nova Scotia	$10.85	$10.85	$847.26
Prince Edward Island	$11.25	$11.55	$819.21
Newfoundland & Labrador	$11.00	$11.00	$1,017.58
Yukon	$11.32	$11.49[1]	$1,053.75
Northwest Territories	$12.50	$13.46	$1,403.08
Nunavut	$13.00	$13.00	$1,275.38

[1] Estimated value following annual adjustment based on change in CPI.
Sources: Minimum wages – Government of Canada; Weekly earnings – Statistics Canada CANSIM, table 281-0027 (Mar. 31, 2016).

According to the data presented in Table 7, the BC minimum rate was about 11% below the national average of $12.79 on March 31, 2017, about 4% below the national average of $11.82 on January 1, 2018, and will remain at that value on January 1, 2019.

There is more wage information in Chapter 37 which compares average wages for a number of specific occupations.

So what do you think after reading this chapter? Does a "Sunshine Tax" exist in Kelowna?

Our research suggests that if Kelowna has a "Sunshine Tax", it is associated with the higher cost of home rental and ownership. Most other cost of living items seem to be lower than in other parts of Canada. Perhaps a portion of the tax is hidden by way of lower earnings in some sectors which we trust newcomers will investigate before making the move to Kelowna.

To save on the cost of living, see Chapter 40 for our trusted business contacts offering discounts on: salon & spa service; automotive & transmission repair; and plumbing & irrigation service.

CHAPTER 13

REAL ESTATE COMPARISONS & TIPS

Purchasing a new home in a new city is very likely the most exciting and anxiety-prone decision one will make when planning a move. This highly emotional endeavour is amplified the farther away one is from their new location. For most folks, the purchase of a home is the biggest and most important investment of their entire life. Add to this, the unfamiliarity newcomers may have with the local market, and you have the recipe for a potentially stressful experience.

Should you buy, or should you rent for a while first, in order to better study the market? Has the market peaked in Kelowna? What if the market crashes or interest rates rise significantly? All of these questions are valid, and all are difficult to answer.

We will be addressing these questions using both statistics (oh joy), and our experience in buying and selling our personal properties since 1989. We are not offering advice on real estate speculating. We prefer to think of our role as one of offering "things to think about before you buy".

National Price Comparison Snapshot

Understanding that real estate prices fluctuate and soon become outdated, we provide Table 1 for baseline and comparative purposes.

Table 1. 2017 Median selling prices (annual % change) of residences[1] in major cities across Canada.

City	Average Selling Price 2016[1]
Vancouver	1,480,712 (12.0)
Toronto	850,899 (17.7)
Victoria	664,482 (18.4)
Kelowna	**637,894 (12.0)**
Canada	626,042 (10.8)
Calgary	479,352 (4.4)
Hamilton	544,399 (22.9)
Ottawa	422,533 (6.8)
Edmonton	386,532 (2.3)
Saskatoon	377,222 (-2.2)
Regina	329,366 (-1.7)
St. John's	327,438 (-2.0)
Halifax	319,891 (4.2)
Quebec City	299,250 (1.8)
Winnipeg	296,907 (3.9)
St. John	206,134 (-0.6)

[1] Aggregate of 2-storys, bungalows, and condos.
Source: [2]Royal LePage 2017 4th Quarter House Price Survey.

Will Your Real Estate Investment Grow?

Investing in real estate is similar to that of investing in the stock of public companies. A key metric in both decisions is "growth". One would be wise to purchase stock in a company whose industry is growing more than other industries. For example, the tech industry is a growth industry. Similarly, one is usually rewarded for buying real estate in a growing real estate market.

In our chapter covering demographics, we learned that in 2016, Kelowna was the third fastest growing city in BC and the sixth fastest growing city in all of Canada. It seems clear that the local real estate market is supported by a trend of significant population growth.

As for future growth, in the fall of 2016, the Canada Mortgage and Housing Corporation (CMHC) made the following predictions for the Kelowna CMA:

- A significant increase in multiple-family housing starts along with steady construction of single-detached homes will result in a higher number of total housing starts in 2016 with some moderation in 2017 and 2018.
- MLS® sales will end the year at a new record level followed by some moderation over the forecast horizon. MLS® average prices are expected to increase significantly in 2018, partially as a result of a shift towards more high-end sales, followed by more modest gains through 2019.
- Population growth is expected to remain steady while employment is expected to pick up, supporting housing demand.

Is Kelowna in a Real Estate Bubble?

Of course anything is possible. Experts from the Bank of Canada and the CMHC have been saying that the Canadian housing market is overvalued for the last couple of years. As a potential newcomer, such predictions will undoubtedly give you pause. We all hate to buy anything that could potentially take a downturn soon after. Memories of what happened to home prices during the Great Recession of 2008 are still vivid in most people's minds. Perhaps it's better to rent a home or even postpone moving to Kelowna altogether?

Oh, what a conundrum, especially given that vacancy rates are nearing 0%. Yes, that is correct. At this time, the Orchard City virtually has no rooms at the Inn. It sounds like the party is over and it's best to stay put. Or, we could look at some facts which might help us come to a more enlightened decision.

1. *Real estate is a cyclical industry.* There have been ups and downs in all markets since Confederation. Even professional real estate

speculators don't always time the market correctly. The chance for non-professional consumers to predict an exact peak is slim at best.

2. *We've been through worse*. It's hard to imagine a more catastrophic situation than that of the financial crisis beginning in late 2007. Even so, the average selling price in Kelowna dropped only 9.7% during this correction. Can you live with that? In general, Kelowna real estate is more resilient than most other locations in the country. This is because of the following points.

3. *Kelowna is a horse of a different color.* Few can argue that Kelowna isn't a great place to live, for all of the reasons covered in this book. These reasons are unlikely to change and, in some cases, will even improve. In addition, there are a number of significant changes to our city which attract and keep people here. Our universities attract domestic and foreign students alike, and the burgeoning growth of the tech sector provides development in high-paying jobs which helps attract and keep young people. Not to sound too dramatic, but it's like a coming of age as Kelowna transforms from a primarily agricultural, service, and retirement community to a more diverse, and dare we say, metropolitan area.

4. *40% of the Kelowna area is in the ALR.* This means that developers must either move up the hillsides (at greater cost to develop and service); increase the density of current properties (which is happening with increased multi-family units, infills and legal suites); or build skyward (increasing condo and apartment towers). This lack of available land for development adds upward pressure on property prices and therefore mitigates the effects of a possible bursting of a real estate bubble.

5. *Demographics are changing*. Seniors still find Kelowna a great place to retire, however the exciting buzz among community leaders today is that the millennial demographic, those born between 1982 and 2004, is increasing rapidly. Unfortunately

we must rely on anecdotal information at this time, but the consensus is that retirees and millennials alike are looking to call Kelowna home.

6. *The Kelowna population is growing.* As mentioned above, experts suggest that Kelowna's above-average growth rate is expected to continue for at least a couple more years. Population growth (demand), coupled with no place to rent (supply), results in higher home prices, which results in more building, which leads to more jobs, and so on.
7. *Vancouver has an affordability crisis.* Even though Kelowna home prices are rising, it is still much more affordable for young people to buy a home here. Interestingly, we have met people who commute to Vancouver from Kelowna on a weekly basis. Such is the strong desire to be able to own a home.
8. *Investment demand is high.* Many savvy real estate investors look to invest in markets where the vacancy rate is less than 1%. Now that this level has been met, more and more multi-family buildings are being built. In fact, such a low rate puts upward pressure on home prices of all types as people scramble to buy rental properties.
9. *Local economy firing on all cylinders.* Economic growth is the catalyst for long-term prosperity and stability in any type of market, and real estate is no exception. We will discuss various economic factors in Part Three.

The above factors bode well for continued long-term growth in the Kelowna real estate market. Furthermore, Kelowna seems to weather the inevitable downturns much better than most other Canadian locations.

The Question on Everyone's Mind - Where to Buy?

Kelowna is large enough to have very distinct neighbourhoods, and most newcomers solicit advice from friends, family or work associates regarding suitable locations. Those who don't have such valuable contacts must rely on the opinion of their realtor, combined with their own research.

Every neighbourhood has its pros and cons and, rather than allowing our personal biases to interfere with your decision making, we have decided to let the chart below do our talking. If you think about it, the average selling price takes into consideration all the factors that one considers important when choosing a neighbourhood, including views, traffic, parks, schools, noise, shopping, crime etc. Table 2 shows the comparative average selling prices for different types of residences within Kelowna real estate submarkets. We have also included a corresponding submarket (neighbourhood) map for your convenience (Fig. 1).

Table 2. Submarket average selling prices, December 2017 ($000's).

Submarket	Single Family Dwelling	Condo	Townhome
Kettle Valley	1,000	*	514
Upper Mission	954	*	656
Crawford Estates	889	*	*
Wilden Estates	854	*	550
Lower Mission	852	348	593
SE Kelowna	835	*	689
Dilworth Mountain	834	278	621
University District	720	349	484
Black Mountain	710	*	486
Glenmore	665	287	464
Joe Rich	652	*	*
Kelowna South	643	338	479
Kelowna North	605	429	550
North Glenmore	602	280	450
Rutland North	546	241	330
Rutland South	508	257	318
Springfield/Spall	490	338	414
Ellison	486	*	643

Source: adapted from Okanagan Mainline Real Estate Board price graphs 2017.
*Insufficient data.

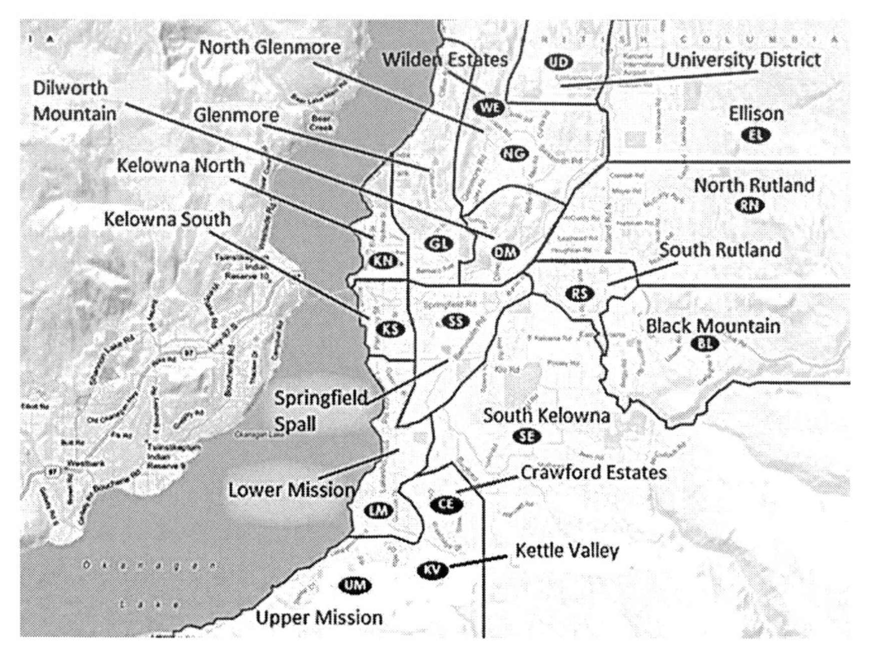

Figure 1. Submarkets of Kelowna. Map courtesy of swproperties.ca.

General Buying Tips

Following is a list of things to take into consideration when viewing properties. We have tried to list items that are somewhat unique to the Kelowna area.

1. *ALR*: The Agricultural Land reserve is defined in Chapter 5. As mentioned, 40% of the Kelowna area is in the ALR. We revisit this topic so that potential home buyers understand that while the parcel of land next to the one that you are viewing might be a beautiful forested patch of nature today, it may not always remain this way. Sure, it is unlikely that a high-rise apartment building or a supermarket will be on the other side of your fence, but it is likely that the forest/grassland will be replaced by apple trees or vineyards, or a herd of cattle. If such a potential change is not an issue for you, by all means go ahead and purchase the property. If you do though, please don't complain when the propane cannons bang early in the morning to scare the starlings away from the grapes, or when farmers spray their crops, or when you

are held up by slow-moving farming equipment. Oh, and by the way, there is nothing quite like the aroma of cattle dung on a wet spring morning.

2. *Check Zoning:* We must stress the need for newcomers to confirm the zoning status of adjacent vacant/undeveloped properties. It can be disconcerting to discover that your neighbour has the right to extract gravel from their property, potentially resulting in a very dusty and/or noisy place to live.

3. *Crown Land*: This is land (or land covered by water-like rivers or lakes) that is owned by the provincial government. It is available to the public for many different purposes, including crop and livestock production and certain commercial development. Most people believe that if they back onto Crown land it will never be commercially developed. While this may be true in general, the point is . . . never say never, and remember that the general public will always have access, right up to your back fence.

   Crown land uses may include quarries; airports; wind farms; golf courses; cell towers; resort developments; residential developments; roads; and various utility lines.

   Additional things to consider when buying property that backs Crown land is the risk of visitation from lawful intruders such as rodents (marmots, mice, voles), insects (grasshoppers), weeds (many types), and wildlife (coyotes, mule deer, black bear, raccoons, bobcats, and the odd cougar).

   Considering all of the above factors, living adjacent to Crown land can be very enjoyable for the informed newcomer who enjoys easy access to nature.

4. *Fire Risks:* Common sense dictates that the closer one is to the outskirts of residential areas, the higher the risk of being impacted by a forest fire. The Okanagan Mountain Park fire of 2003 consumed over 25,000 hectares of forest and park land

south and east of the city, forcing the evacuation of more than 27,000 people and destroying 239 homes on the southern edges of the city. The good news is that experts suggest that this type of inferno is a one-in-a-hundred year occurrence.

5. *Wild Fire Covenants*: Be aware that in many new subdivisions developed since the 2003 fire, local municipalities have mandated that Wildfire Covenants be registered against title to the newly-created lots. A Wildfire Covenant is an agreement between a landowner and a municipality which defines the limitations, conditions and restrictions on the land. Some of these restrictions and conditions include no wood shingles, no planting of conifer trees, and the removal of dying or dead trees in order to lower the risk of wildfire.

6. *Suites*: Due to the extremely low vacancy rate, Kelowna City Council has relaxed regulations for secondary suites in all residential areas, except Gallagher's Canyon. This may be a good thing however, if you need a lot of parking space, be aware that multiple residents next door may take a spot or two.

7. *Snow Levels*: It may surprise many newcomers that it is not uncommon to get a significant dump of snow in higher elevation neighbourhoods such as Upper Mission or Dilworth Mountain, only to drive down to the "flats" and find no snow at all. If it is important for you to minimize the amount of snow that you will have to shovel, you may wish to stick to neighbourhoods in the valley bottom.

   Newcomers should understand that from October 1st until March 31st, motorists who drive on the valley's main corridors and Highway 33 are required to install winter tires (with snow flake symbol). Drivers who fail to do so risk a fine of $121.

8. *Traffic*: Although this topic is covered in more detail in Chapter 39, you may wish to consider your route to work and/or school when looking for a home. One area which experiences major

congestion and potential delays is the Upper Mission. There are only two exit roads from this densely-populated area. Line ups and wait times can be long, especially after a snowfall.

9. *Native and Private Land Leases*: If you come across a beautiful large home, on a great lot, at what seems to be an incredibly low price, be aware that it is likely on leased land. You would be buying the right to live on the property for say, 99 years, but you will not own the land.

10. *Lake Front Living*: Oh, just the thought makes one green with envy toward those that can afford a home that is just steps from the beach. Not to sound like sour grapes, but even lake front locations have potential issues to consider. One is that living on the lake during the winter months can be dreary, wet and bitterly cold when the wind is up. Foreshore homeowners should also be prepared to protect their property in the event of high lake levels, as occurred in 2017 (See Chapter 6).

    Another point to understand is that the public has the right to walk the entire shoreline of Okanagan Lake without impediment from fences or other structures. This can be particularly concerning the closer you are to Bennett Bridge, as summertime visitors often spend the night very close to (or even in) your yard.

11. *Sewer or Septic:* Approximately 80% of Kelowna properties are serviced by sewer lines leading to the city's waste water treatment plant. The other 20% are served by septic systems made up of a holding tank and a distribution field, often located in the front yard of the property. It is important to be educated on how the system operates, how old the field is, and how to maintain it.

    A family of four is looking at about $400 every 3 years to have their tank emptied. A typical septic "field" in good drainage soil is supposed to last about 20 – 30 years.

Our two experiences with septic systems:

In 1995, we had to pay about $7,000 to replace our septic field and a little landscaping. It was about 15 years old and we were told that was the average life of a field located in loamy soil areas where drainage is an issue. In March of 2017, we were notified that sewer installation on our street will begin in two weeks. They need to go down 4 m and thus the cost estimate is $22,000!... Sure hope this book sells.

We had to replace our field four years after moving in. We never thought to ask how old the field was. We were told by the City that sewer wouldn't arrive to our street for about 10 years, so we had it replaced for about $5,000. One year later the City decided to hook-up our area to the existing sewer line and it cost almost $8,000 for us to do so. Very frustrating (and expensive).

Lessons learned – ask how old the field is, and be sure to find out where the tank and its opening are located. Many people landscape over their tank and lid, making it difficult to locate when the time comes to clean it out.

We would be remiss if we didn't point out the difference between "sewer hook-up" and "sewer installation". A sewer hook-up refers to the connection from your home out to the middle of your street where the sewer trunk line is buried. Our experience suggests that one should budget about $2,000 for this service.

A sewer installation refers to areas where the homes and streets are already in place but the underground sewer trunk line is not; therefore, the existing streets must be dug up and the sewer pipe installed. This is not an inexpensive proposition. The cost range for residents in this situation is about $3,000 for easy-access, high density sub-divisions, and up to $48,000 for difficult to access, low-density subdivisions. Apparently, one can pre-pay the full amount or have the cost added to their tax bill and make annual payments over 20 years.

This topic is important for newcomers to investigate when looking for a property. If the home you are interested in is on a septic system, it is worthwhile to contact Kelowna City Hall to determine the sewer installation schedule for your location, and ask for an estimate of the costs involved.

12. *Swimming Pools:* It is worth confirming that permits for swimming pools, hot tubs and out-buildings are in place. In the swimming pool business, it was not uncommon to see pools encroaching on a setback to a property line which required that the pool had to be moved, or it would be removed.

    By the way, if you are interested in a home with a pool, Kelowna has many to choose from. In fact, about 20% of Kelowna homes have pools which is four times the average in BC.

13. *Steep Driveways*: Many homes designed to take advantage of lake and mountain views are built on mountain sides and, inevitably, they have very steep driveways. This is no problem in summer, but during winter it can be quite stressful and even dangerous descending down an icy sloped driveway.

We trust that the information provided in this chapter will help you make a more informed decision about how and where to buy a residence in Kelowna.

See Chapter 40 for our trusted business contacts offering discounts on: home inspections; home cleaning; mortgage consulting; and swimming pool services.

CHAPTER 14

RENTAL ACCOMMODATIONS ... OR LACK THEREOF??

It was mentioned earlier that there was "no room at the Inn" in Kelowna, and now it's time to address this point. The downside of rapid population growth is that it creates a significant challenge for those looking for rental accommodations. Until the market corrects this situation by building more rental units, this challenge will continue.

The following statistics are from the October 2017 Canada Mortgage and Housing Rental Market report. This data refers to the primary rental market, which only includes rental units in privately initiated apartment structures containing at least three rental units.

Overall Kelowna Vacancy Rate	Overall Average Rent
0.2%	**$1,043**
Decreased by 67%	Up by 8.6%

How Can This Be?

The CMHC attributes the continued tightness in the rental market over the past two years to a significant increase in rental housing demand outpacing supply, the rising cost of homeownership relative to rents, rising enrolment in post-secondary institutions, strong population growth and growing employment opportunities for young people.

The low vacancy rate is in part attributable to the significant increase in net migration to the Kelowna CMA which increased from a net gain of 2,191 people in 2013 to an estimated gain of 3,425 people in 2015. Between 2011 and 2016 census years, the population of the Kelowna CMA has grown 8.3% compared to the national average of 5.0%.

Additionally, the trend in full-time employment among individuals between the ages of 15 and 24 years, while initially moving downward following the commodity price shock of late 2015/early 2016, has made a strong recovery through 2017 (Statistics Canada - Labour Force Survey).

Finally, the Kelowna area population growth has resulted in greater competition in the resale market which has been characterized by higher sales, lower active listings, and stronger increases in average MLS® prices of all housing types. Given the elevated price growth in the existing home market, some potential new homeowners may have decided to delay their purchase while choosing to remain in rental accommodations, contributing further to demand for rental housing.

As the size of the primary apartment rental universe expanded by only 289 units between October 2016 and October 2017, rental demand likely shifted to rental condominiums and other secondary market options. But help is on the way. In 2018, an estimated 1,500 new rental units are being added to Kelowna's inventory of 14,000. This addition is expected to increase the vacancy rate to about 2.1%, which is still tight. The average rent for a two-bedroom condominium increased 2.8% between October 2016 ($1,478) and October 2017 ($1,519).

How Does Kelowna Compare?

Table I compares Kelowna's overall vacancy rate and average rent of primary rental units (apartments and townhouses) to other major Canadian cities. You can see that Kelowna has the lowest vacancy rate (0.2%) in all of Canada. This lack of supply is a very tight market for rental availability and, as a result, the cost of renting an average space has risen substantially over the past year (8.6%). Kelowna ranked 7th highest among the listed major cities for average monthly rent in October 2017.

Table 1. Vacancy rates and average monthly rent for selected Canadian cities, October, 2017.

City	Overall Vacancy Rate	Overall Ave. Rent $/mo
Vancouver	0.9	1,297
Toronto	1.1	1,296
Calgary	6.3	1,128
Ottawa	1.7	1,113
Edmonton	7.0	1,101
Victoria	0.7	1,072
Kelowna	**0.2**	**1,043**
Halifax	2.3	1,027
Regina	7.0	1,026
Hamilton	2.4	1,020
Saskatoon	9.6	999
Winnipeg	2.8	970
Canada	3.0	947
St. John's	7.2	866
Quebec City	4.5	793
Montreal	2.8	766
St. John	4.7	713

Source: CMHC Rental Market Survey Report, October 2017.

Table 2 shows the average rental rates and % change from October 2016 to October 2017 for apartments and condominiums in Kelowna.

Table 2. Average rent by rental and bedroom type and annual % change.

Rental Type	Bachelor	1 Bdrm	2 Bdrm	3 Bdrm
Apartments	861 (21%)	943 (8.6%)	1,179 (8.7%)	1,289 (2.6%)
Condominiums	nd	nd	1,519 (7.8%)	2,275

Source: CMHC Rental Market Survey Report, Oct. 2017. nd = no data.

Clearly the 'Inn' has few rooms and, unfortunately, the cost is likely to move higher, at least until construction of more rental units catches up to demand.

See Chapter 40 for our trusted business contact offering architectural design services for multi-family housing and commercial construction projects.

CHAPTER 15

WILL MY FAMILY BE SAFE?

Another important question on the minds of most newcomers relates to the safety and security of one's person, family and property. The prevalence of crime is not a statistic that cities care to broadcast. However, we feel this subject must be addressed so that you can judge for yourself if Kelowna offers the security you require to live here with confidence. In this chapter we will describe the current status of crime in Kelowna compared to the latest provincial and municipal crime statistics.

Figure 1 illustrates that on a national scale, BC, along with the Prairie Provinces, has an intermediate level of crime.

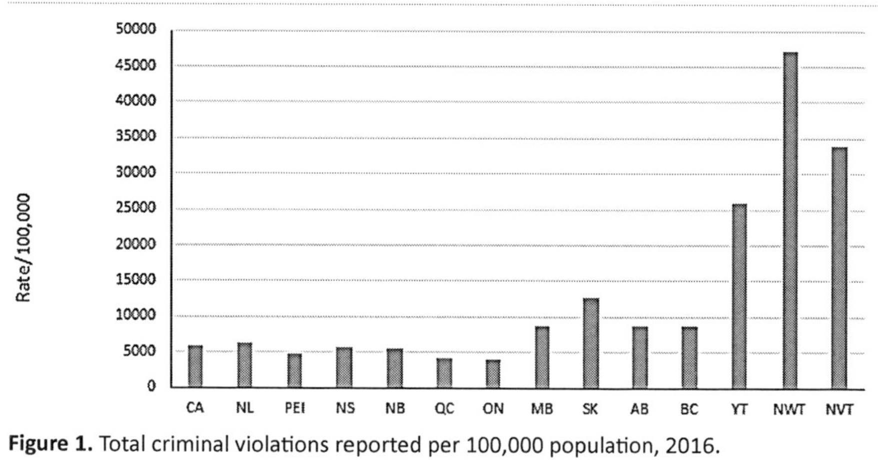

Figure 1. Total criminal violations reported per 100,000 population, 2016.
Source: Statistics Canada, CANSIM table 252-0051, 2017-07-24.

Turning our attention now to Kelowna crime statistics, Table 1 highlights four incriminating crime-related results. First is the comparative

2016 crime rates for CMAs across Canada; second is the percent change in the crime rate from 2006 to 2016; third, the Total Crime Severity Index (TCSI); and finally, the Violent Crime Severity Index (VCSI). Unfortunately Kelowna does not score well on two of these important metrics. Between 2005 and 2016, the actual crime rate decreased by 27% which was just below the national average. Of the 34 CMAs reporting, Kelowna had the 3rd highest overall crime rate, but only a 2% increase over 2015. The national crime rate did not increase over the same period. It appears that not only do we have an elevated crime rate (8,445), but the severity of those crimes is worse (100.3) than the national average (71.0).

Table 1. Police-Reported Crime Statistics (per 100,000) by CMA.

CMA	2016 Crime Rate	% Change 2006 to 2016	Total Crime Severity Index[1]	Violent Crime Severity Index[2]
Regina	9,253	-25	125.8	124
Saskatoon	8,942	-26	117.8	114
Edmonton	8,131	-16	105.7	102
Winnipeg	6,653	-40	103.9	150
Kelowna	**8,445**	**-27**	**100.3**	**63**
Vancouver	7,282	-28	94.3	73
Thunder Bay	6,259	-29	85.9	126
St. John's NL	5,721	-15	79.2	89
Calgary	5,260	-20	74.6	61
Canada	**5,224**	**-28**	**71.0**	**75**
Victoria	5,689	-42	63.8	57
Halifax	4,663	-46	61.0	77
Montreal	3,389	-44	57.8	73
Kingston	4,743	-27	55.2	38
Guelph	4,496	1	54.6	49
Ottawa	3,492	-37	51.3	62
Quebec City	3,000	-36	45.2	51
Toronto	2,954	-34	47.5	70

[1] Crime Severity Index (CSI) measures both the volume and seriousness of reported crime incidences and has a base index of 100 for 2006.
[2] Violent crime refers to those violations in the Criminal Code identified as crimes against the person.
Sources: Statistics Canada, CANSIM tables 252-0051 and 252-0052; Canadian Centre for Justice Statistics, Uniform Crime Reporting Survey.

The TCSI is a relatively new measure that takes into account not only the number of crime incidences, but also the relative severity of each incidence based on length of incarceration and type of crime. As Table 1 shows, Kelowna's 2016 crime rate dropped by 27% since 2006. Although Kelowna was ranked third for crime rate and fifth for TCSI, it did not rank in the top 10 CMAs for Violent Crime Severity Index. In fact, Kelowna's VCSI (63) was 16% below the national average (75).

Results of an analysis of Statistics Canada's 2016 municipal crime data by staff of Maclean's magazine and posted online March 2018 revealed Kelowna ranked as the 34th most dangerous city among the 229 cities with populations over 10,000. Kelowna ranked in the top 10% only for drug trafficking (excluding marijuana) (14th), and in the top 20% for fraud (25th), cocaine trafficking (30th), breaking and entering (33rd), and impaired driving (45th).

Figure 2 presents how the number of criminal code offences (property, person and other) has changed in Kelowna since 2013.

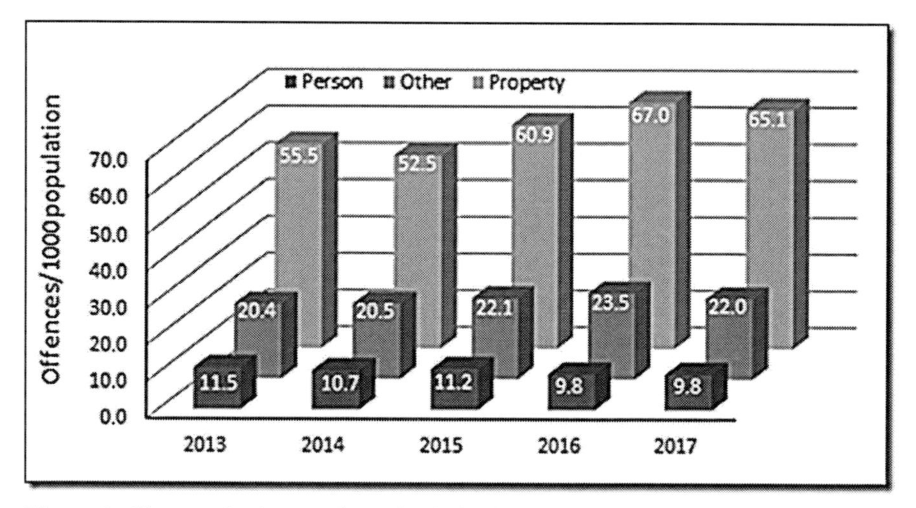

Figure 2. Changes in the number of criminal code offences/1000 population in Kelowna, 2013-2017.

Source: RCMP Q4 Report to Kelowna City Council, 19 February 2018.

Offences to person have decreased almost 15% whereas offences to property and other criminal code offences increased by 18% and 17%, respectively.

Increasing drug-related violations are generally associated with increases in property theft, as noted above. To combat this unfortunate phenomenon, the RCMP is very proactive and tenacious in its enforcement actions to put those selling drugs out of business. This leads to a higher number of arrests and convictions which is reflected in Kelowna's high ranking in reported drug offences. Eventually the drug dealers will learn Kelowna is not a safe place to do business!

Kelowna and area is also a victim of the opioid crisis affecting the lives of thousands of people across Canada. Based on data posted by the BC Coroners Service, the City of Kelowna had the 3rd highest rate (59.0) of overdose deaths per 100,000 population (2016) among the 15 largest cities in BC in 2017.

Kelowna contracts its policing services to the Royal Canadian Mounted Police. In 2017 there were 185 members headquartered in Kelowna who were supported by 55 auxiliary staff. They deliver their services from local offices in Peachland, Big White, Lake Country, West Kelowna and two neighbourhood offices in Kelowna. According to Statistics Canada, in 2016 there were 190 officers per 100,000 population across Canada. The ratio for the Kelowna area was 135.

Of the 22 cities with populations between 100,000 and 200,000 reported by Statistics Canada, the average number of police officers was 143 per 100,000 population. Kelowna compares favourably with cities of similar population size but has room to grow to achieve the national average.

Beginning in 2017, social workers will accompany patrols in the downtown area to better help street people avoid criminal entanglement. Other initiatives will include summer bike patrols, introducing a bait bike program (similar to bait car), Don't be an Easy Target educational campaign to reduce thefts from cars, increasing visible presence in hot spots, monitoring movements of known offenders, and working with businesses to improve security. A new $48 million police headquarters was officially opened in June of 2017 in order to accommodate the increasing staff levels and services.

The forgoing may sound downright scary, however it seems that residents are not concerned. A 2017 Citizens Survey conducted for the City of Kelowna by Ipsos Reid revealed that 90% of respondents said the city was safe, and 94% agreed their quality of life was good or very good.

In the same survey, fewer than one in 20 mention crime as an issue, nearly all respondents considered Kelowna a safe community, and most respondents considered the police services as one of Kelowna's primary strengths. Credit for this level of confidence in personal safety must be attributed where it is due, and that is the professional policing services provided by the RCMP.

CHAPTER 16

WILL MY PETS BE WELCOME?

Both of your humble authors have been pet owners in the Kelowna area for a combined forty-five years. The rules and regulations surrounding pet ownership have definitely become more stringent, particularly over the last couple of years. Even so, the Okanagan is generally quite pet-friendly, albeit in an organized and regulated manner.

Most newcomers to the area might assume that dog control is a matter governed by our City Fathers, as is likely the case in other parts of Canada. In fact, it is the Regional District of Central Okanagan (RDCO - see Chapter 4) which is responsible for the administration and enforcement of the Responsible Dog Ownership Bylaw No. 1343. The RDCO is contracted do this on behalf of the City of Kelowna. Their website, regionaldistrict.com is quite helpful and easy to navigate.

Understanding that most people don't relish the idea of reading the legalese inherent in bylaw statements, we have paraphrased a few rules most applicable to newcomers:

1. You must license your dog within 30 days of becoming a resident.
2. Once your dog has had its three-month birthday, it must be licensed every year, even if it never leaves your home. The fine for no dog license is $300 with zero tolerance.
3. Residents are permitted to house up to three dogs over the age of three months.
4. Owners can transfer a valid dog license from another jurisdiction. ☺

5. All dogs in public places must be kept on-leash held by the owner. The only exception is an off-leash dog park. Fines for off-leash violations are $150 for the first offence.

6. Dog excrement is not allowed on any property other than the homeowner's property, and even then it must be removed in a timely manner. The fine for failure to pick up dog excrement is $150.

License fees for most dogs in the RDCO for 2017/2018 are actually quite reasonable. Your spayed female or neutered male is $20/year and unspayed or unneutered dog is $60/year, if paid before March 1. On or after March 1, the fee for a spayed/neutered dog is $40.00 and $80.00 for an an unspayed/unneutered dog. Failure to follow the regulations will result in fines that can be onerous. Please refer to the RDCO website regionaldistrict.com, for more details on the cost of dog by law infractions.

The licensing of cats within in the RDCO is not required, although the topic has been raised by some residents, especially avid gardeners.

Off-Leash Dog Areas

There are seven permanent and two temporary off-leash dog areas listed on the City of Kelowna website. They are open every day from 6:00 a.m. until 11:00 p.m.

Permanent Areas	Glenmore	1250 Glenmore Road N.
	Ellison Fields	4680 Old Vernon Road
	Enterprise Way	2500 Enterprise Way
	Knox Mountain	450 Knox Mountain Drive
	Duggan Park	1494 Bernard Avenue
	Mission	3975 Gordon Drive
	Cedar Creek	5200 Lakeshore Road
Temporary Areas	Rowcliffe Park	536 Rowcliffe Avenue
	Vancouver Recreation Park	375 Hartman Road

According to the 2016 Canadian Dogs Annual magazine of The Redstone Media Group in Peterborough, ON, Kelowna ranked first out of 50 Canadian cities for being pet-friendly.

They used eight different criteria to rank each city, first assessing the numbers per capita. Criteria included the numbers of veterinarians, pet-sitters, trainers, and pet supply retailers, as well as pet-friendly accommodations, pet-friendly restaurants, dog parks or beaches and air quality in each city. Each criteria were ranked per category, and then weighted from one to five, based on importance. The website states:

> *"Top Dog" honours go to Kelowna, BC. Located on the eastern shore of Okanagan Lake, this city ranks in the top ten in four of our categories. Along with having the best air quality out of all the Canadian cities we looked at, Kelowna ranked highly in the off-leash dog park category. There's even a brochure, complete with maps, available to download on the city website. Kelowna ranked number two position for pet-sitters.*

Kelowna SPCA (Society for the Prevention of Cruelty to Animals)

The Kelowna SPCA is an active and modern facility located at 3785 Casorso Road in the south eastern part of the city. This location is easily accessible and is in close proximity to some great walking areas for members of the public who wish to take the SPCA residents for some exercise. They are open 7 days a week from noon to 4:30 p.m.

Kelowna SPCA adoption fees include spay/neuter (or discount for the operation if it has not been done prior to adoption), a health check, and vaccinations.

Adult Dog	$299.00
Small Breed Adult Dog	$399.00
Mature Dog (over 8 years old)	$149.50
Puppy (under 6 months)	$399.00
Mature Cat (over 8 years old)	$57.50
Adult cat (under 8 years old)	$115.00
Kitten (under 6 months)	$145.00

In BC, all SPCA cat/kitten/dog/puppy adoptions include a microchip and the companion animal must be registered with the BC Pet Registry.

Other Animals

The City of Kelowna states in Bylaw No. 8767 that *"the keeping of animals and poultry other than household pets is prohibited in all zones in the City."* There are exceptions to this regulation especially in certain agricultural zones where the lot sizes are deemed appropriate.

The Bylaw 8767 stipulates which zones and lot sizes permit animals such as rabbits, poultry, horses, cattle sheep, goats or combinations thereof. There has been plenty of debate over this topic in recent years. It wasn't long ago, for example, that you would find your neighbours with rabbits, chickens or even the odd goat in their back yards. These days, however, the regulations and enforcement is much more restrictive.

Suffice it to say, potential newcomers with a desire to keep farm-type animals should refer to the City of Kelowna website and become familiar with which areas allow non-household pets before they purchase or rent a property. It is not enough to rely on advice from friends, family or even your realtor.

Pet ownership is very popular in Kelowna. Pets are most welcomed and accommodated in our city, however owners are expected to be responsible and respectful.

See Chapter 40 for our trusted business contact offering a discount on pet boarding.

CHAPTER 17

FAITH ORGANIZATIONS

Faith organizations play an important and active role in Kelowna life through ministering not only to congregations, but also to the less fortunate in the city.

Following the arrival of Father Pandosy in 1859 and construction of the first chapel in Kelowna (now the Immaculate Conception Parish), many more settlers arrived along with their various faiths. This eventually led to construction of more churches as congregations grew larger and more prosperous. The earliest churches constructed include the Bethel Presbyterian Church in 1892 (now Benvoulin Heritage Church), the first Anglican Church in 1895 (where the current Kelowna Museum now stands), St. Andrew's Anglican Heritage Church in 1911(also includes a cemetery), the First United Church in 1910, and the Cathedral Church of St. Michael's and All Angels in 1913.

Today, Kelowna is home to 73 church congregations, four temples and one synagogue. Does that sound like a lot of places of worship for a city of our size? Well, let's have a look at a few similarly sized cities across Canada and see how Kelowna compares (Table 1). We checked individual city websites for estimated population data as of December 2016.

Table 1. Number of places of worship per 1000 population.

City	Population	No. Places of Worship	Places of Worship/1,000
Abbotsford, BC	143,000	83	0.58
Kelowna, BC	**127,380**	**77**	**0.60**
Regina, SK	223,000	144	0.64
Saskatoon, SK	262,900	156	0.59
Thunder Bay, ON	109,140	96	0.88
Barrie, ON	154,283	62	0.40
Guelph, ON	128,000	62	0.48
Ajax, ON	134,530	32	0.23
Whitby, ON	136,377	29	0.21
Kingston, ON	156,023	78	0.50
St. John's, NL	106,172	63	0.59

Source: Yellow Pages.ca listings of churches and other places of worship, Dec. 2016.

The fact that Kelowna was just above the average of 0.57 churches per thousand population for the cities listed suggests it is typical for cities of its size for the number of places of worship.

Table 2 lists the variety of denominational faiths active in Kelowna. There are also at least seven non-denominational organizations. Kelowna is the headquarters for both the Roman Catholic Diocese of Nelson and the Anglican Diocese of Kootenay.

Table 2. Religions with places of worship in Kelowna.

Anglican	Ecankar	Pentecostal
Baha'i	Evangelical Missionary	Presbyterian
Baptist	Free Methodist	Roman Catholic
Buddhist	Gospel Hall	Serbian Orthodox
C3 Church	Jehovah's Witness	Seventh-Day Adventist
Calvary Temple	Jewish	Sikh
Christian & Missionary Alliance	Latter-Day Saints	Ukrainian Greek Orthodox
Christian Reformed	Lutheran	Unitarian
Christian Science	Mennonite	United
Church of the Nazarene	Muslim	United Slavic

According to Statistics Canada, 53.9% of Kelownians reported affiliation with a Christian denomination, followed by 42.9% who reported no religious affiliation (Table 3).

Table 3. Total population in private households by religion.

Religion	Total Population 176,435	% of Total Population	% of Christian
Buddhist	695	0.4	-
Christian	95,175	53.9	-
Anglican	9,410	-	9.9
Baptist	6,305	-	6.6
Catholic	27,610	-	29.0
Christian Orthodox	1,355	-	1.4
Lutheran	5,360	-	5.6
Pentecostal	3,325	-	3.5
Presbyterian	1,475	-	1.5
United Church	12,855	-	13.5
Other Christian	27,480	-	28.9
Hindu	505	0.3	-
Jewish	430	0.2	-
Muslim	555	0.3	-
Sikh	1,870	1.1	-
Aboriginal Spirituality	205	0.1	-
Other religions	1,500	0.9	-
No religious affiliation	75,495	42.8	-

Source: tistics Canada, 2011 National Household Survey.

Given that Christianity is the largest reported denomination, we thought it would be interesting to see how other CMAs compare for this denomination. These results can be viewed in Table 4.

Table 4. Proportion of total population reporting Christian or no religious affiliation for selected CMAs.

CMA	Total Population	% Christian	% No Affiliation
Vancouver	2,280,695	41.7	41.4
Kelowna	**176,435**	**53.9**	**42.8**
Calgary	1,199,125	55.6	32.4
Regina	189,745	67.8	27.1
Winnipeg	650.000	63.7	28.7
Toronto	5,521,235	56.7	21.1
Ottawa	1,215,735	70.0	20.8
Montreal	3,752,475	74.4	14.9
Halifax	384,540	71.5	24.9
St. John's	193,830	89.9	8.8

Source: Statistics Canada, 2011 National Household Survey.

Over the years, many Christian churches have come together to sponsor refugee families from war-torn nations. The most recent sponsorships involve families from Syria and other nearby nations.

Several congregations have outreach programs or collaborate with other social service agencies to help the local homeless and marginalized people.

Faith organizations in Kelowna play a very active and vital role in ministering not only to the spiritual growth and needs of their congregations, but also to the less fortunate, both here and abroad.

CHAPTER 18

ABORIGINAL POPULATION & LANDS

According to Statistics Canada's 2016 National Household Survey, 6.0% (11,370) of the population of the Kelowna Census Metropolitan Area (CMA) had an Aboriginal identity. Of those, 46.0% (5,235) reported a First Nations identity only, 49.6% (5,645) reported a Metis identity only, and 1.2% (140) reported an Inuit identity only. An additional 140, or 1.3%, reported other Aboriginal identities and 210, or 1.8%, reported more than one Aboriginal identity.

It can be confusing at times to identify the lands owned and managed by our aboriginal friends. Figure 1 below should help clarify things for newcomers.

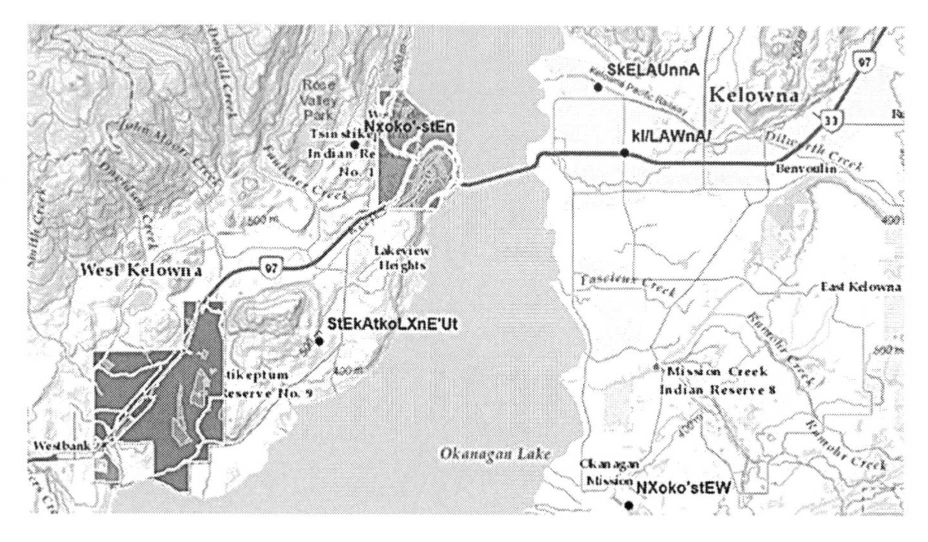

Figure 1. Location of Westbank First Nations reserve lands within the Kelowna CMA.

The Westbank First Nation (WFN) comprises five reserves totaling 2,161 hectares (5,306 acres). The two populated reserves, Tsinstikeptum Reserves 9 and 10 (dark areas on map), border Okanagan Lake and are somewhat intermingled within the City of West Kelowna boundaries. The remaining three reserve areas are located on the east side of Okanagan Lake in the Kelowna area and lie in unpopulated areas.

On April 1, 2005 the WFN became one of the first Aboriginal groups in Canada to achieve self-government. This status gives WFN greater control and law-making authority over governance, social and economic development, education, health, lands and more.

The information in the next table and the impressive commentary below it are taken from the WFN website.

Number of Band Members	>850
Number of Non-Member Residents	9,000 (approx. 8,000 within IR#9 and 1,000 within IR#10)
Number of Homes	>4,000

As noted above, in 2016, there were 11,370 Aboriginal people in the Kelowna area (CMA – including WFN reserve areas). Aboriginal people make up 6% of the population of the Kelowna/ Okanagan area, slightly more than BC's proportion of 6% and 4.9% Canada-wide. As well, 57.8% of the Kelowna/Okanagan area First Nation people are 'status' as defined under the Indian Act in 2016.

Non-aboriginal residents do not pay property transfer tax on WFN lands but do pay annual property taxes for leased properties. Every three years, leaseholders have an opportunity to vote for and are represented by Advisory Council district representatives. Through this mechanism, residents may provide input towards Westbank Law and proposed amendments, developments, budget preparations and tax rates.

WFN's leadership is comprised of one Chief and four Councilors elected by WFN Band Membership every three years.

Westbank First Nation is an economic leader among First Nations in Canada, building wealth for the community and valuing the role of business in generating its independence, wealth and long-term success. With an entrepreneurial-spirited membership, a history rich in culture and tradition, diversity in employment, strong commercial and residential sectors, along with healthy forestry and tourism industries, and an Economic Development Commission providing linkages between government, members and businesses, WFN continues to bring forward annual statements showing healthy profits and capital re-investments back into the community.

CHAPTER 19

LGBT2Q+ COMMUNITY

Our LGBT2Q+ (lesbian, gay, bisexual, transgender, 2-spirit, queer and additional identities) community is lead and organized by a group called the Okanagan Pride Society.

We reached out directly to their current President and Director of Communications to give us some insight into their history, objectives, and accomplishments. We have included their response below.

The Okanagan Pride Society was established in June 1996 and is a non-profit organization based in Kelowna that is committed to serving the Okanagan's LGBT2Q+ community. The organization values and supports individuals, families and allies; creates events; and offers programs to connect our community and advocate for equity, inclusion and acceptance within the Okanagan Valley and beyond. Okanagan Pride is a catalyst for building and celebrating the strength, equality, dignity and self-determination of the LGBT2Q+ community in Kelowna and throughout the Okanagan.

The organization's purpose is to:

- Provide opportunities for the LGBT2Q+ community in Kelowna and beyond to meet, provide support for each other, socialize, celebrate and create community in safe spaces and settings.
- Foster partnerships and build alliances across communities that advance equality and acceptance of the LGBT2Q+ community.
- Support and assist a peer support group for LGBT2Q+ youth to provide a safe, confidential and accepting space empowering

them to discover who they are, to celebrate their diversity, to realize their immense worth.

- Promote and foster the Pride movement as a vehicle to celebrate equality and diversity, engender community support, and make the Okanagan a safe and accepting place for the LGBT2Q+ community.
- Bring our voice to the global community in support of equality and diversity regardless of sexual orientation or gender identity.

The Okanagan Pride Society is consistently sought after to provide educational opportunities within the community. We work with professionally trained mental health facilitators in a variety of outreach activities— community group presentations, gender and literacy training for the workplace, and facilitating requests for LGBT2Q+ resources and materials.

PART TWO

Is Kelowna A Fun And Interesting Place To Live?

"IT IS GOOD PEOPLE WHO MAKE GOOD PLACES."
ANNA SEWELL, *BLACK BEAUTY*

Chapter 20

MAY AS WELL START WITH NUMBER ONE

Beaches, parks, and water activities is the number one category cited by visitors in 2016 when asked by Tourism Kelowna how they plan to spend their time during their visit to Kelowna (Fig. 1). Add boating to this category and you will clearly understand the importance of water-related activities as a key attraction to this area.

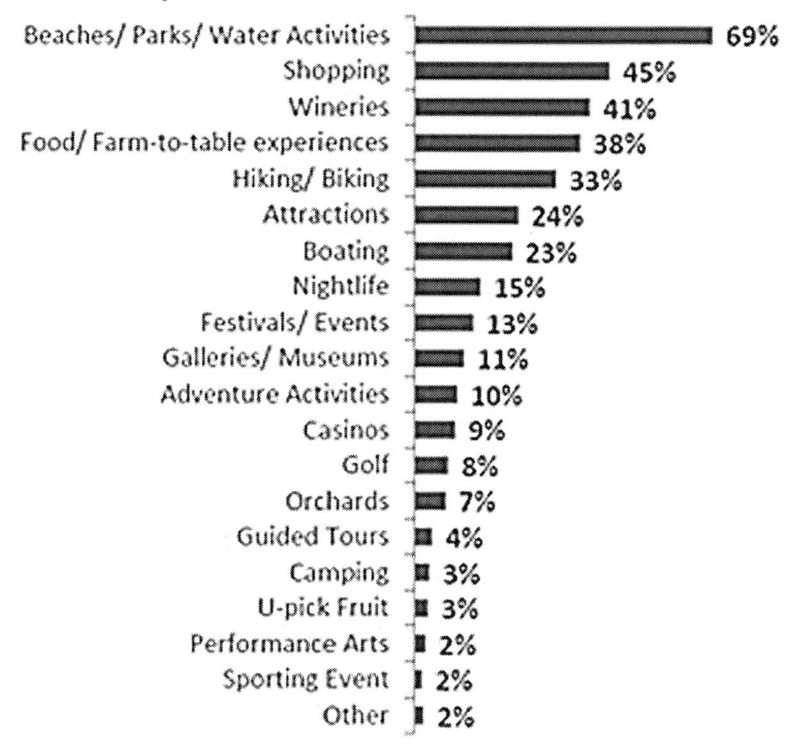

Figure 1. Most favourite activities reported by tourists to Kelowna.
Source: Tourism Kelowna Visitor Intercept Survey, March 2017.

Now you may be wondering, as we were, 'what about downhill skiing, snowboarding and Nordic skiing?' The answer is, "the timing of the survey is spring through fall and therefore the study did not capture that type of data."

Kelowna has nine swimming beaches within its city limits; that's about 13,700 people per beach. In comparison, Toronto, the largest city in Canada, has eleven swimming beaches or about 255,000 people per beach. Vancouver has nine beaches with about 67,100 people per beach. It is highly likely that Kelowna has the most beaches per capita in the entire country. This provides lots of room for residents and visitors alike.

Tourism Kelowna does a great job in describing all nine of our sandy beaches. Unless otherwise noted, dogs are not permitted on public beaches.

- *Cedar Creek Park:* Long and narrow off-leash, dog-friendly pebble beach with picnic tables and portable washrooms on site. Cedar Creek is Kelowna's only off-leash dog friendly waterfront park.
- *Boyce-Gyro Beach:* One of Kelowna's most well-known beaches. Equipped with snack venues, a rope swing, volleyball courts, playgrounds, inflatable waterpark, water sport rentals, picnic areas and washroom facilities.
- *Hot Sands Beach - City Park:* Long sandy beaches, volleyball and basketball courts, grassy fields, playground, waterpark, skateboard park, washroom and change room facilities, on-site rentals. Live music during summer months (Parks Alive!) as well as local vendors and buskers. Although on-leash dogs are permitted on the boardwalk and pathways, dogs are not permitted on this beach.
- *Kinsmen Park:* Located next to the waterfront (water access for swimming but no sandy beach). Tall leafy trees, large grassy areas, picnic tables, tennis courts, washroom facilities.
- *Rotary Beach Park:* This park offers designated swimming areas, change rooms, playgrounds, picnic areas, shady trees and on-site rentals - a popular spot for kite-surfers.
- *Sarson's Beach Park:* This neighbourhood beach's smaller size gives the park a homey feel. On-site playground, picnic tables, designated swimming areas and washroom facilities are offered.
- *Strathcona Park:* Located next to the Kelowna General Hospital, Strathcona Park has designated swimming areas, sandy beaches,

picnic tables, public washrooms and kid's playground all surrounded by tall oak trees and a large grassy area.

- *Sutherland Bay Park:* Sutherland Bay Park sits at the base of Knox Mountain with grassy fields, a kid-friendly playground, tennis courts, boat-launch, and washroom facilities. Dogs are welcome here on-leash. Swimming at Sutherland Park is not recommended due to poor water quality.
- *Tugboat Bay - Waterfront Park:* Sandy beaches, beautifully landscaped gardens, washroom facilities, paddle boat rentals and boat launches. Close to restaurants, shopping, nightlife, as well as live music on the Waterfront Park Stage during summer months. Although on-leash dogs are permitted on the boardwalk and walkways, dogs are not permitted on this beach.

Please note that none of these beaches are patrolled by lifeguards.

Abundant and clean fresh water is a tremendous asset for residents and a clear winner for visitors. If we remain good stewards of our lake, it will remain a source of enjoyment for many decades to come.

Chapter 21

WINE – FROM THE VINEYARD TO THE BOTTLE

One of the many factors people consider when deciding to move to Kelowna is the proximity to locally produced, award-winning wines. Perhaps this is one of the reasons you are making the move. Well, you won't be disappointed. Kelowna has some very interesting wineries and great wines to satisfy the most discerning wine connoisseur. In fact, the Okanagan Valley has been named the #1 wine region in North America (Huffington Post) and voted by consumers as the #2 wine region to visit in the world (USA Today). This chapter will briefly describe the development of the local industry and how it evolved to deserve such prestigious accolades.

As mentioned in Chapter 1, the French Catholic priest, Father Charles Pandosy, planted the first vineyard in the Kelowna area in 1859 to provide grapes to make sacramental wine. The grapevines were *Vitis labrusca* (known as fox grape) which are native to eastern North America and thus hardy enough for the cold winters.

Other small vineyards were soon planted so that local wineries could be supplied. This prospered until the early 20th century when prohibition caused the industry to collapse. When prohibition ended in the 1930's, the industry got back on its feet and from then until the 1970's, various wines were produced. These included *V. labrusca* and hybrid grapes (e.g. Marechal Foch and Vidal Blanc), berries, apples, cherries and table grapes.

Calona Vineyard Winery opened in 1932 and is BC's oldest continuously operating winery. Let's be honest, the table wines and related products produced during that time were certainly no competition for foreign wines.

Plantings of *Vitas vinifera* grapevines began in earnest in the 1970's using European cultivars bred to withstand Kelowna winter temperatures. Momentum increased in the late 1980's when Canada entered into the North American Free Trade Agreement that allowed western US wineries to sell their wines in Canada. In response to the increased competition from American wines, the Canadian government implemented a vine replant program with grants to help growers replace their hybrid and *V. labrusca* vines with *V. vinifer*a vines. With the switch to *V. vinifera* varietals, Kelowna wineries were able to produce much higher quality wines that could compete with European and American imports.

The British Columbia Wine Institute lists the Kelowna-Central Okanagan as one of eight viticultural regions in the Okanagan Valley. Okanagan Lake has a moderating effect on the local climate such that cold snaps are short-lived in winter, and the long hot summer days provide grapevines with the heat and sunlight necessary to produce excellent grape vintages. The heavier soils vary in the content of sandy loam, clay and gravel compared to the deeper sandy soils in the South Okanagan.

All local wineries participate in the BC VQA (Vintners Quality Assurance) created in 1990 to certify that BC VQA-labeled wines meet specific standards with respect to the origin, vintage and varietals. At present there is almost an even split between red (51%) and white (49%) wine production.

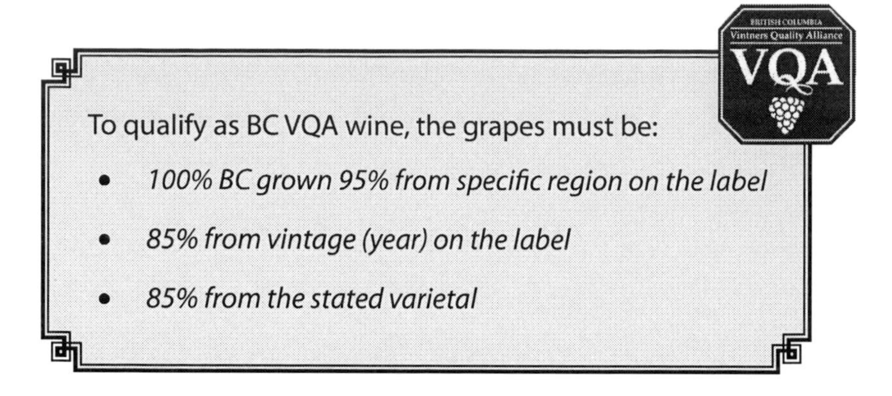

In addition to the traditional red and white wines, local wineries also produce bruts (same as champagne), sparkling rosés, and world-famous BC Icewine (also known as dessert wine). Wineries sell directly to customers from the on-site wine shops/tasting rooms, through BC VQA Wine Stores, government and private liquor stores. With recent changes in interprovincial liquor sales legislation, BC wineries can now market their wines in most provinces across Canada.

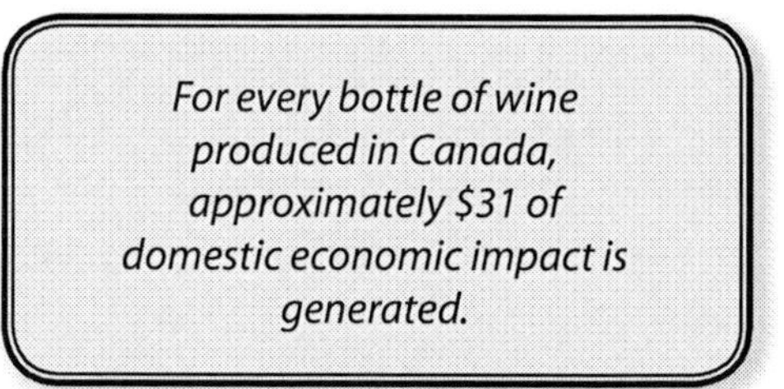

Icewine is a special category of BC VQA and its production is highly regulated in BC in order to protect the integrity of the process and the "Icewine" term. Only prescribed *V. vinifera* or Vidal Blanc varietals are used. Grapes are picked frozen when the temperature is less than -8° C (17.6° F) and crushed while they are still frozen so the sugars are concentrated. Only the sweeter grape juice is collected. Oher standards must also be met to have the product labeled as BC Icewine. The higher labour costs and risks to the grapes (birds, diseases, drying and drop) involved in making a relatively small amount of wine make icewines more expensive than regular table wines. If you don't mind being on call to work in the dark at temperatures below -8° C, then you are invited to leave your contact information with an icewine winery before November. According to a local vineyard manager, pickers are required on short notice because grapes must be picked as soon as the temperature falls below -8°C. To add to the work load, bird netting must be removed just before the grapes are picked.

Kelowna Winery Listings

Table 1, along with the corresponding map, lists all wineries located in Kelowna. Please note that addresses are included so that they can be easily loaded into your GPS.

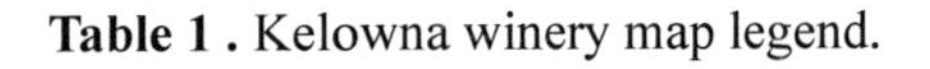

Table 1 . Kelowna winery map legend.

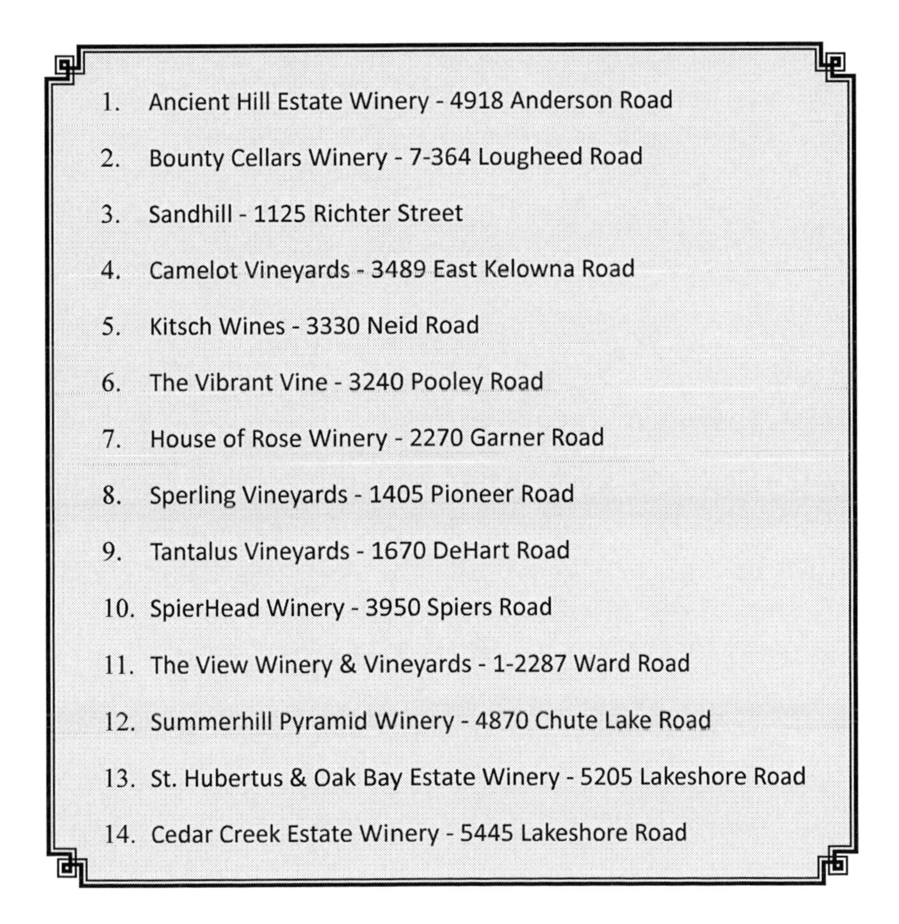

1. Ancient Hill Estate Winery - 4918 Anderson Road
2. Bounty Cellars Winery - 7-364 Lougheed Road
3. Sandhill - 1125 Richter Street
4. Camelot Vineyards - 3489 East Kelowna Road
5. Kitsch Wines - 3330 Neid Road
6. The Vibrant Vine - 3240 Pooley Road
7. House of Rose Winery - 2270 Garner Road
8. Sperling Vineyards - 1405 Pioneer Road
9. Tantalus Vineyards - 1670 DeHart Road
10. SpierHead Winery - 3950 Spiers Road
11. The View Winery & Vineyards - 1-2287 Ward Road
12. Summerhill Pyramid Winery - 4870 Chute Lake Road
13. St. Hubertus & Oak Bay Estate Winery - 5205 Lakeshore Road
14. Cedar Creek Estate Winery - 5445 Lakeshore Road

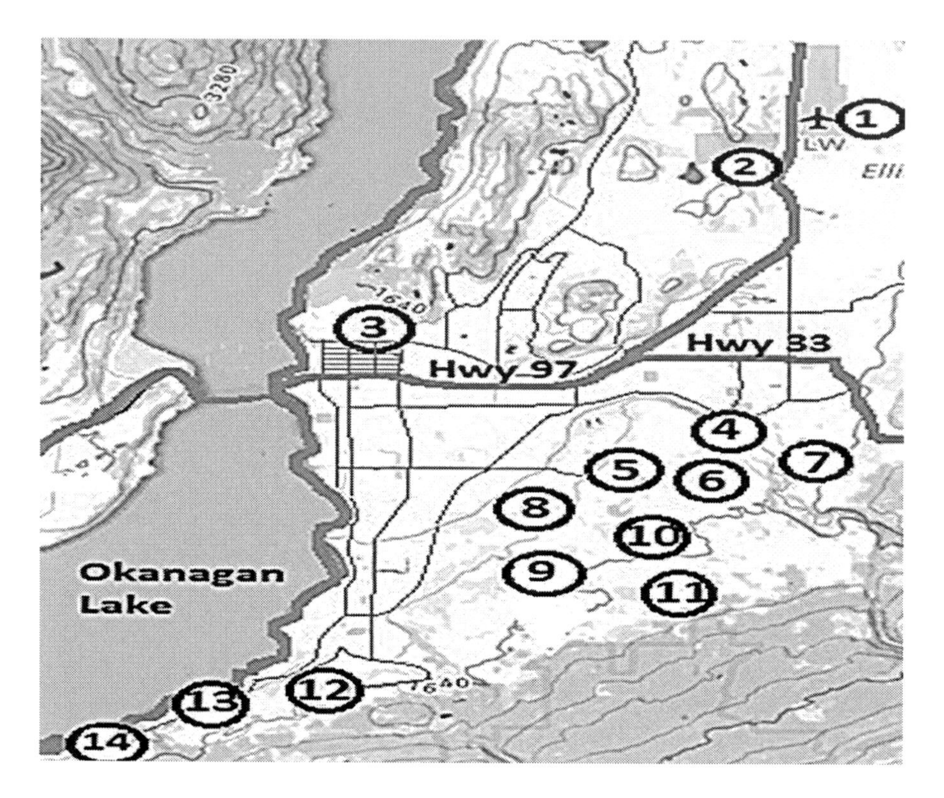

Figure 1. Map of Kelowna wineries.

West Kelowna Winery Listings

West Kelowna is home to 15 more wineries that are within a 30-minute drive from downtown Kelowna. Refer to the list and map locations below. Similar to many Kelowna wineries, grapes are often sourced from the South Okanagan and Similkameen valleys where the climate and/or soil is more favourable for certain varietals.

Table 2 . West Kelowna winery map legend.

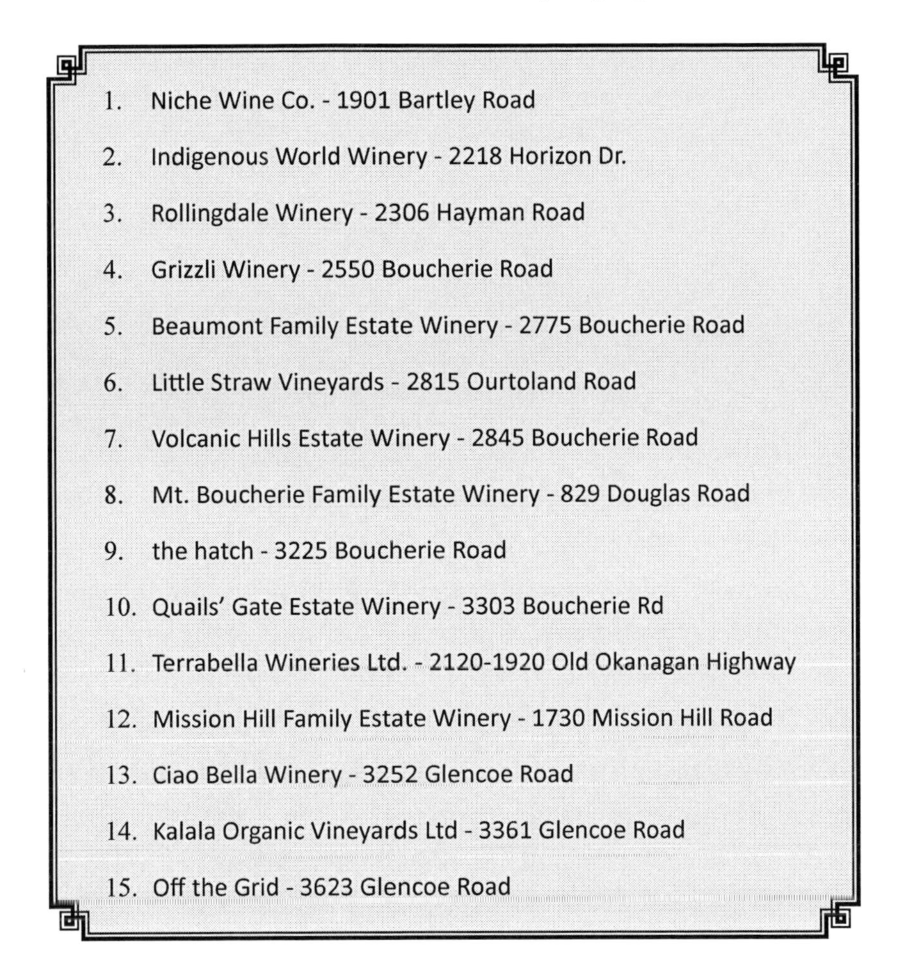

1. Niche Wine Co. - 1901 Bartley Road
2. Indigenous World Winery - 2218 Horizon Dr.
3. Rollingdale Winery - 2306 Hayman Road
4. Grizzli Winery - 2550 Boucherie Road
5. Beaumont Family Estate Winery - 2775 Boucherie Road
6. Little Straw Vineyards - 2815 Ourtoland Road
7. Volcanic Hills Estate Winery - 2845 Boucherie Road
8. Mt. Boucherie Family Estate Winery - 829 Douglas Road
9. the hatch - 3225 Boucherie Road
10. Quails' Gate Estate Winery - 3303 Boucherie Rd
11. Terrabella Wineries Ltd. - 2120-1920 Old Okanagan Highway
12. Mission Hill Family Estate Winery - 1730 Mission Hill Road
13. Ciao Bella Winery - 3252 Glencoe Road
14. Kalala Organic Vineyards Ltd - 3361 Glencoe Road
15. Off the Grid - 3623 Glencoe Road

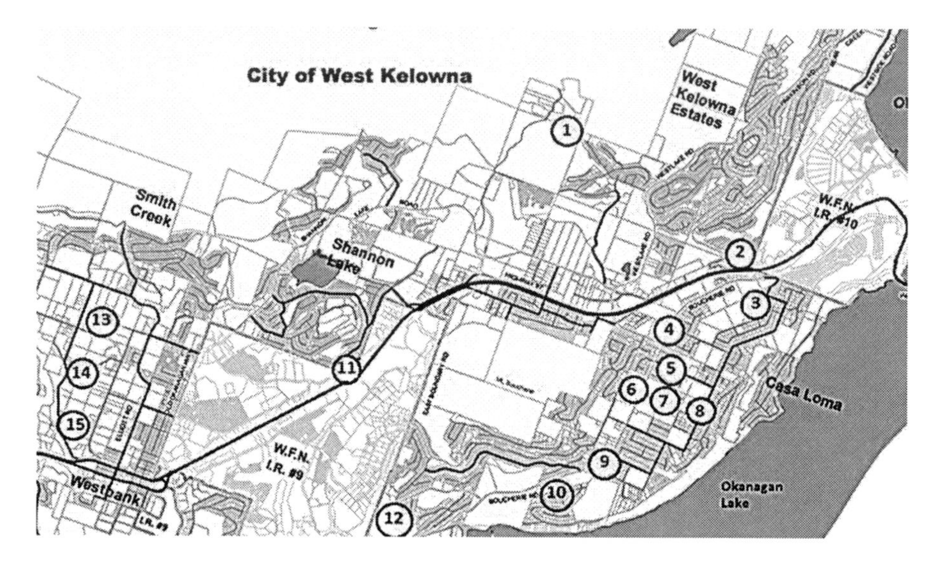

Figure 2. Map of West Kelowna wineries.

According to data reported in the 2014 BC Wine Institute annual acreage report, there were 85 vineyards (9% of total valley vineyards) in Kelowna and West Kelowna, growing about 30 different cultivars of wine grapes on 420 ha (1,037 ac) of land (10% of total valley ha).

There are two major events each year where one can taste the wine from many of the aforementioned wineries. One is the 10-day Spring Wine Festival in early May, and the other is the Fall Wine Festival in early October.

A good reason to visit each winery individually is that not all local wines are sold through the government liquor stores, restaurants, farmers' markets or private beer and wine stores. A 2016 survey of wineries by Orchard and Vine Magazine revealed 93% of respondents sold wine through their tasting rooms, 88% through restaurants, and 88% through private beer and wine stores compared to only 43% reporting sales through government liquor stores.

When visiting a winery for taste-testing, be prepared to encounter plenty of other visitors and potential line-ups, especially when a bus load of tourists descends on the winery. Wineries in the Central Okanagan are within comfortable driving distance of each other, so you can take visiting friends and family to a good selection of wineries in a short time. If you plan to sample a lot of wines, a safer alternative is to hire one of the many local wine tour operators to tour you around. You will learn about the industry and how grapes are produced and processed. Also, you will receive tips on how to better appreciate your tasting experience.

So let's raise our glasses to the grape growers and the wine makers, and toast to their continued success.

CHAPTER 22

CAN'T WAIT TO PLANT MY OWN FRUIT TREES

> *Almost 30% of the Southern Interior apple and pear production area is within the city limits of Kelowna!*

There is nothing quite as enjoyable as picking ripened fruit from your own tree and savouring the wonderful flavour and sweetness. One of the first things new residents undertake when they settle into their homes is to plant one or more fruit trees. Unfortunately, most newcomers are not aware of the work involved in maintaining fruit trees, nor are they fully informed when they purchased the trees. Because of the large residential-orchard interface in the area, urban fruit tree owners must make every effort to prevent the development and spread of insect pests and diseases to nearby commercial orchards.

To help reduce the prevalence of pests and diseases in backyard fruit trees, the Regional District of Central Okanagan (RDCO) enacted the Noxious Insect and Pest Infestation Control Bylaw No. 879 (2000) that requires fruit tree owners to control certain noxious insect pests and diseases. Enforcement actions are initiated following receipt of a complaint. The RDCO enforces the bylaw throughout the district, including Kelowna.

The three Okanagan regional districts, along with the Columbia-Shuswap Regional District, are partners with the tree fruit industry in the operation of the Okanagan-Kootenay Sterile Insect Release Program (OKSIR). This area-wide integrated pest management program aims to keep codling moth (the worm in the apple/pear) below levels that require sprays. The OKSIR program has the authority to have apple, pear or crabapple fruit removed or trees cut down if the tree owners fail to control codling moth. All property owners pay a small tax to support the operational costs of the program which has reduced codling moth numbers by over 95%.

The following table, derived from the BC Tree Fruit Production Guide, lists the number of common diseases and insect and related pests that attack fruit trees in the Okanagan Valley. Although fewer in number, if left uncontrolled, diseases can directly or indirectly lead to the death of trees. As a fruit tree owner, you are responsible for ensuring that your trees are not a source of the listed pests and diseases.

Tree Fruit	Insect and Related Pests	Diseases
Apple	32	7
Pear	28	2
Apricot	17	4
Cherry	25	3
Peach/Nectarine	10	4
Prune/Plum	18	1

Fruit tree owners have several options to avoid creating insect pest and disease problems:

1. Do not plant fruit trees. Plant trees that do not host tree fruit pests and diseases. Use the money saved to buy local fruit.
2. Hire a licensed pest control operator to apply control products.
3. Control pests and diseases yourself using appropriate and effective methods, including sprays.

The loss of effective control products available for personal use has made it much more difficult to control most insect pests and diseases. Licensed pest control operators are authorized to use more products that effectively and safely control pests and diseases.

The effective control of fruit tree pests and diseases requires the proper application of other management practices such as proper fruit thinning, tree pruning, and fertilizing. New fruit tree owners often find it difficult to properly thin fruit, but in not doing so, the ripe fruit will be much smaller and at greater risk of insect and disease damage.

These management practices must be supported by weekly inspections, and an immediate response is required in order to prevent development of pest/disease problems. As a courtesy to neighbours, always inform them when your trees are to be sprayed so they can close open windows and take other measures to avoid exposure to accidental spray drift.

If the maintenance of your fruit trees becomes too onerous, remove some or all the trees – don't abandon them. Your neighbours and nearby commercial growers will be most appreciative!

CHAPTER 23

GREEN THUMBS UP

This chapter is for newcomers who enjoy participating in one of the most popular physical activities in Canada – gardening. According to the Canadian Fitness & Lifestyle Research Institute's 2014-2015 Physical Activity Monitor report, gardening or yard work was the second most popular activity among Canadian adults.

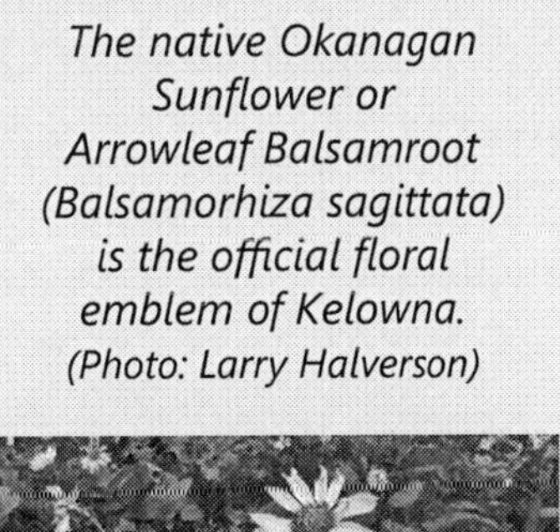

The native Okanagan Sunflower or Arrowleaf Balsamroot (Balsamorhiza sagittata) is the official floral emblem of Kelowna. (Photo: Larry Halverson)

Kelowna has a wonderful climate to grow a wide variety of plants to create interesting and varied gardens and landscapes. Newcomers must be cautioned, however, because Kelowna is located in a semi-arid climatic zone which means:

- low summer rainfall
- periods of high summer temperatures

There are hundreds of local native plants that the Syilx people used as food, medicine, art, and clothing. Okanagan College, in collaboration with the Westbank First Nations planted the Nn'k'wulamen Garden in 2017 to showcase 50 native plants of cultural significance to the Syilx people.

Kelowna is in Plant Hardiness Zone 7a which means plants must be able to survive temperatures as low as -15.0°C to -17.8°C. This rating should only be used as a comparative guide as other factors can impact how well plants thrive if not accustomed to the climate. Proximity to Okanagan Lake (colder further away and higher) is a major factor. For example, fruit trees blossom almost one week earlier in Vancouver than in the Lower Mission area which is located within three blocks of the lake. The latter area, however, generally enjoys a longer frost-free period than areas further away from the lake because of the lake's moderating effect.

Keeping in mind the low summer rainfall and high summer temperatures, gardeners have landscape design, planting and maintenance options to accommodate these extremes. For example, in 2017 Kelowna gardeners witnessed the 4th highest spring precipitation levels, followed by the hottest July and August on record, along with no rainfall.

According to the Okanagan Basin Water Board (OBWB), 24% of Kelowna's water supply is used for outdoor purposes, with lawn and gardens being the thirstiest of the many uses. Although Okanagan Lake appears to be a huge supply of fresh water, the yearly resupply of water from all precipitation is only 1.5 m (5 ft.) and only 15% of this resupply is available for our use. This gives the Okanagan Valley the distinction of having the lowest available resupply of water per capita in Canada; however, Kelowna residents use almost twice the national average amount of water per day.

About 50% of outdoor water use in Kelowna is over and above what is required to maintain an attractive property.

In addition to introducing water meters in 1996 and user-pay water rates in 1998, the city introduced year-round water use restrictions in 2016. Odd and even numbered properties can only water on 3 different days of the week (none on Monday). Automatic timer sprinkler systems are restricted to between midnight and 6 a.m. up to 3 days per week.

Manual sprinkling is restricted to between 6 a.m. and 10 a.m. and between 7 p.m. and midnight up to 3 days per week.

Residents must make an application to the City to install any new or renovated landscape irrigation system to areas over 100 m^2 (1076 sq. ft.) For most residents this means hiring expertise to develop the irrigation plan and to complete the landscape water conservation checklist and calculation table.

Two major ways to reduce summer water usage regardless of your watering system is to:

- eliminate or minimize the lawn area, and to
- use plants that have reduced supplemental water needs.

You can reduce your water usage by replacing lawns with several different kinds of non-plant cover or drought-tolerant ground cover. You can also incorporate native plants and drought-tolerant plant species. This type of landscaping, called xeriscaping, is gardening within the limits of the local environmental conditions and using adapted local plant species. It does not mean excluding water for plant maintenance. Water is used only to supplement rainfall based on the needs of the plants. The Okanagan Xeriscape Association has an excellent website that provides information on how to plan, install and maintain a xeriscape.

Another informative website for both experienced and novice gardeners is the Kelowna Garden Club, one of the largest in BC. Once you have finalized your landscape plans, we highly recommend you attend the club's annual spring plant sale at Guisachan Heritage Park. You can buy plants reared by members under Kelowna conditions and you can speak to established local gardeners.

According to our vegetable growing friends, you can grow more than enough varieties of veggies, berries and, of course, fruit trees and grapes. For those who do not have access to space for a vegetable garden, you can join ($30 annual fee) the Central Okanagan Community Gardens Society. The Society has constructed raised garden beds at 16 sites around the city where gardening members are assigned a plot in which to grow their vegetables (maximum one plot per household). You can visit the society's website for more information on membership.

In 2008, the City passed Bylaw No. 9920 to regulate the use of pesticides for non-essential (i.e. cosmetic) purposes. What this means is that no homeowner may apply a pesticide on their property for the purpose of preventing, controlling or suppressing infestations of pests (insects, mites, diseases, weeds) which affect outdoor ornamental plants or turf. Basically, you cannot apply any pesticides to protect the cosmetic appearance of plants or lawns. There are a number of pest control companies in Kelowna with trained, certified staff to apply pesticides.

The City encourages the planting of trees to help expand and sustain a healthy urban forestry canopy across the city. To this end, the City operates a NeighbourWoods Program each spring whereby residents can purchase a limited supply of selected trees including maple, lilac, oak, pine and mountain ash at a reduced cost.

The City of Kelowna lists the following trees as generally less desirable for landscape planting for the reasons mentioned.

- Boxelder Maple (Manitoba Maple) – messy, host for home-invading Western Boxelder bug
- Tree of Heaven – invasive (spreading)
- Birches – short-lived, drought intolerant, top dieback
- Indian Bean – messy (seed pods, large leaves)
- Lawson's Cypress– prone to root disease
- Poplars– short-lived, weak-wooded, prone to rots, root sprouting, falling limbs
- Siberian Elm – weak-wooded, weedy, messy (seeds, leaves)
- Willows – weak-wooded, messy (leaves, flowers), drought intolerant

We would also add:

- Female Honeylocust – large seed pods
- Trumpet Vine (or creeper) – spreads by roots

The City of Kelowna Glenmore Landfill accepts yard waste (grass and hedge clippings, leaves, tree prunings less than 5 cm in circumference, flowers, but no sod or soil) for a fee of $5.00 up to 250 kg (550 lbs.). For new residents arriving from colder regions, you will be amazed at how much yard waste is produced each year; this of course will depend upon how many trees (especially fruit trees) and shrubs you have that require annual pruning. Grass clippings should be mulched when mowed and left on the lawn to decompose. As a word of caution, be sure to cover and secure your load with a tarp in accordance with local bylaws, or face a fine of $150.

All the yard waste is chipped after removal of non-plant material, then composted on-site to make GlenGrow. Yard waste is also used to produce OgoGrow at the Regional Compost Facility by composting it with biosolids, hog fuel and wood ash. Application of these products to lawns and gardens aids in weed control, water retention, and improves soil tilth, organic content and fertility. You can purchase both products at the landfill. Check the City of Kelowna Glenmore Landfill web site for current pricing.

Regardless of residence type, location, or property size, all gardeners will find that Kelowna offers tremendous opportunities to apply their skills and imagination to create beautiful landscapes.

CHAPTER 24

WILDLIFE - FEATHERED AND FURRY FRIENDS, OR FOES?

Many newcomers to Kelowna are sometimes overwhelmed by the number and varieties of creepy-crawlies that invade their gardens and homes. However, once you move here, you may soon discover that your property is also under threat by much bigger, albeit cuter/cuddlier critters, that don't creep or crawl.

Birds of a Feather

We will start with some of our feathered visitors. Depending on the data source, birders have reported between 309 and 485 species of birds in the Central Okanagan. The Kelowna area provides many different habitats for birds where birders can spend hours anytime of the year looking for common and rare birds. If you are lucky, you may set a new bird record.

Some of our feathered friends can be a real nuisance. We have listed some common examples below:

- California Quail: loves certain seedling plants like young leafy vegetables.
- Starling: invades attics; takes over other birds' nests and bird boxes; eat/damage ripe tree fruits and grapes; very messy.
- Northern Flicker: pecks holes in wood and plaster siding.
- American Crow: loves to open exposed plastic garbage bags and spread contents; fledged youngsters can be very noisy calling to parents for food first thing in the morning.
- Great Blue Heron: loves any expensive koi or cheap goldfish it can pull out of garden fish ponds.
- Canada Geese: droppings foul beaches and adjacent lawns, golf courses and parks; can increase *E. coli* bacteria in recreational water to dangerous levels.

These birds are but a small portion of the many species we can all enjoy on our walks and hikes. Just remember to take your bird book and binoculars. Oh, and yes, Kelowna has a Christmas Bird Count.

You Dirty Rat!

Yes, Kelowna has rats! This rodent has arrived only recently and is unlike the monsters you may have heard of or seen in other cities (especially port cities).

The black (or roof) rat is gradually spreading into neighbourhoods throughout Kelowna as it finds suitable accommodation and food to enjoy. It looks like a grey squirrel but without the bushy tail. This rat invades structures for shelter and nesting after feeding on whatever food they can find (pet food, tree fruits and nuts, bird seed, food scraps, insects, snails and slugs). The key to preventing intrusion (or getting rid of them) is by preventing access to shelter, food and water; a very tall order, but necessary.

The roof rat measures 18-20 cm (7-8 in.) and it is twice the length of some of these other smaller rodents:

- Field Vole: 10 cm (4 in.) long, stocky body with short tail and ears and lives in weedy or grassy areas;
- House Mouse: 5-10 cm (2-4 in.) long, narrow body, pointed ears, long tail; and
- Deer Mouse: 8-10 cm (3-4 in.) long body, greyish with white belly, and lives mainly in forested areas (much less common).

The Tree Rat

When we moved to Kelowna almost 30 years ago, we were so pleased to have our own walnut and hazelnut trees from which we could harvest nuts each fall. It was about 12 years ago that we noticed some eastern grey squirrels in the area, and all of a sudden we had no hazelnuts to harvest and our walnut harvest dropped by 90%! Also, the chatter of our native cute and friendly American red squirrels has gradually dropped to the point where it is rare to hear them, let alone see them.

Besides walnuts and hazelnuts, the eastern grey squirrel (also has a common black colour variant) enjoys tree buds, berries, seeds and cherries. When these foods are scarce they will feed on small rodents (including other squirrels), frogs, small birds, eggs and even offspring. Cats, raccoons, hawks and dogs will feed on squirrels if captured.

The Bandit

Another four-legged furry critter that loves human habitation is the raccoon. We have to admit there are few baby animals cuter than a young raccoon with its beady little eyes peeking through its bandit mask. Dumpster-divers,

It is ILLEGAL to keep raccoons as pets in BC and to intentionally feed them inside or outside the home. It is also harmful to the animals themselves.

pond-raiders, garden-destroyers, night-raiders are just some of the printable monikers applied to this mainly nocturnal scavenger.

Raccoons share the same food taste as the black rat, but prefer to add a bit more protein by snatching any insects or fish that can be dug up or captured. This animal is to be tolerated, not feared. Raccoons do not carry rabies, but can carry a roundworm that is dangerous to people. Raccoons can be a threat to smaller pets, especially when there is a dispute over who gets the pet food.

You cannot get rid of raccoons, but you can discourage this animal by minimizing access to food. Trapping is not an option because other raccoons will soon move in to fill the void. On the plus side, since the arrival of raccoons in the early 1990's to our neighbourhood, we no longer have the occasional odoriferous emission of startled skunks.

Deer☺ or DEER☹

A scene becoming more and more common in Kelowna (well okay, all of Southern BC) is the presence of deer quietly enjoying the bounty of our gardens, then silently leaving after 'dropping' a visitation reminder. For some, this event must be digitally captured at every opportunity (especially if the doe has fawns). But for many more, it means replenishing their deer repellant(s) to save their fruit trees or gardens.

Depending upon where you live, white-tailed deer, or the larger and more predominant mule deer, can appear anytime, anywhere in the city.

Why have deer become a problem in recent years? Increasing urban development in the valley bottoms and lower hillsides is decreasing their natural winter range. Mule deer are also running out of favoured open areas to graze as trees recover after the devastating 2003 forest fire. The deer have found that the city offers a smorgasbord of replacement food choices and is adapting to living in the city year-round.

There are many lists posted online informing gardeners which plants deer will eat and avoid. Our experience has taught us that these lists are only a guide. In many areas pyramidal cedars are called deer candy, but in other areas deer prefer other plants before trying the cedars. We are not suggesting that you ignore the lists, but be prepared to amend it through your own experience.

Once stags have grown their antlers, they love nothing better than thrashing the branches of trees and shrubs to remove the velvet and to note their presence in the area. Small trees and shrubs can be destroyed, and the lower portions of larger ones left looking pretty ragged.

Deer are a major problem for tree fruit and grape growers who must erect a 2.5 m (8 ft.) high gated, page-wire fence around their properties. You don't have that option as a homeowner because residential fences cannot exceed 2.0 m (6.5 ft.) in height. If your property abuts an agricultural or commercial operation, the maximum height is 2.4 m (7.9 ft.), which will greatly reduce deer entry.

What other tactics can you use to discourage deer? Locally, gardeners rely on alternating repellants (e.g. commercial and homemade liquids, dog and human hair, scented hand soap, etc.). Good luck with these! A more effective option is to erect a fence around susceptible garden areas or the whole property using 2.2 m (7 ft.) wide plastic mesh netting. The black mesh fence is much easier to install and is less obtrusive.

We have a word of caution for dog owners. Does with fawns will readily attack dogs, even when on leash. Try to avoid placing your dog and yourself at risk when nursing does are present.

Some communities throughout the Southern Interior have so many deer that gardeners, orchard and vineyard managers are calling for a deer cull. This is a very controversial topic that will ultimately have to be dealt with as more and more deer become urbanized.

What Else is out There??

The following are other wildlife sightings in the city that you should be aware of so you can take precautions to avoid conflicts. Residences closer to the city outskirts are more likely to be visited of course, but it is surprising how far these animals will travel into the city in search of an easy meal.

- Coyote: visits neighbourhoods in search of easy prey such as cats and small dogs.
- Cougar: reports of presence is increasing valley-wide as they hunt for natural prey (deer) in residential areas where the urbanized deer are becoming less cautious.
- Black Bear: occasionally enter neighbourhoods as fall approaches in search of fruit and accessible household garbage.
- Bobcat: very rare and can be a threat to small pets, but will take care of rodents from mice to rats to marmots.

The next creature is neither furry nor feathered but we thought we should mention it as newcomers must be aware of its existence in the Kelowna area. We refer to snakes, and there are six species.

- Western Rattlesnake
- Common Garter
- Great Basin Gopher (often mistaken as a rattlesnake)
- Rubber Boa
- Western Terrestrial (Wandering) Garter
- Western Yellow-Bellied Racer

The Western rattlesnake is the only poisonous reptile on this list. It lives in dry, grassy, rocky, sparsely treed sites in Southern Interior valley bottoms and feeds on small rodents. This snake is rarely found in the city but hikers should be alert when using trails. Rattlesnakes are reclusive and shy, so the risk of a bite is rare unless they are provoked.

A bite is rarely fatal, and in recent years only 3-4 attacks are reported province-wide. The Western rattlesnake is on Canada's Species At Risk List due to its loss of habitat.

Again, we must stress that your chances of ever encountering a snake in Kelowna are extremely low. In 27 years, we have only seen one Garter snake and one Gopher snake, let alone a rattlesnake. One final note, the Gopher snake (also known as a bull snake) will mimic the defensive behaviour of the rattlesnake when threatened by coiling up and shaking its tail.

How many of these feathered and furry guests visit your property will depend in part on where you live in Kelowna, and whether your property offers something these visitors find appealing. We must leave it up to you which you perceive as friend or foe, entertaining or annoying.

CHAPTER 25

INSECTS AND THEIR RELATIVES – RELAX, ONLY ONE TYPE CAN KILL YOU

The climate of the Okanagan Valley is not only attractive to people but also to hundreds of different kinds of insects, spiders and ticks. New residents soon learn they will share their indoor and outdoor space with many 6- and 8-legged creatures. For some, this space-sharing does not bode well for their personal peace of mind.

Is there cause for concern? Which of these creatures can be a worry? How and where do you find them (or they find you)? This chapter will highlight only those that could directly impact you or your residence. Let's start with insects – ants, beetles, butterflies, flies, wasps, etc.

The Stingers

The most dangerous for some people are wasps, hornets and bees because of allergic reactions to stings which can be fatal if not immediately treated. Anti-sting kits are essential for those at risk. Wasps (yellow jackets and hornets) can become very numerous in the late summer and pose a threat wherever they congregate to collect food. These stingers are actually beneficial by feeding on other insects for most of the season.

The smaller, long-legged European paper wasp is very common in the area. It builds very small exposed nests just about anywhere. It is not aggressive but, like other wasps, it will sting if the nest is threatened.

The Bloodsuckers

One of the first things many new residents (especially those from the Prairies) realize is the absence of annoying hordes of mosquitoes. This is especially evident in the late afternoons and evenings when recreational activities are underway. Prairie folk scoff at the locals complaining about being harassed by one or two mosquitoes. There are few areas in Kelowna where sufficient snow melt or rain water collects for long enough to result in mosquitoes becoming a nuisance.

The Home Wreckers

A potential, but little-acknowledged, problem insect is the western subterranean termite. It is native to the Southern Interior where it helps recycle dead plant material such as fallen trees common in the local forests. However, once these natural sources of wood are removed for development, this sneaky termite will turn its attention to the new wood-frame structures. The cost to eliminate termite infestations can run into the thousands. But take heart. It takes many, many years before your house is rendered structurally unsafe by uncontrolled infestations. Still, knowing something is gradually nibbling away at your home can be unsettling.

Western subterranean termite

There are many species of ants present in the Okanagan of which only one group can occasionally cause significant problems – carpenter ants.

Like termites, carpenter ants tunnel into the dried and decaying wood components of buildings, reducing their structural soundness.

The Stinky One

Western conifer seed bug

A common indoor nuisance during the winter is the western conifer seed bug. It invades homes to seek shelter from cold temperatures. Locally it is called 'the stink bug' because it emits a disagreeable odor when handled roughly or squashed. You can easily hear its wings beating as it slowly flies around a room looking for a place to land. It is harmless to plants, people and pets, and does not harm outdoor conifers (pine, spruce, fir, juniper, and cedar).

Turning to **non-insect** threats, the two most common are the black widow spider and the Rocky Mountain wood tick.

The Widow Maker

Black widow spider

There are several species of spiders in the Okanagan but only the black widow spider can cause an illness which is rarely fatal, but can have painful symptoms. Fortunately these shiny black spiders are very timid and reclusive, and human cases of black widow bites are very rare.

The hobo spider is a common brown, ground-dwelling spider that has an undeserved reputation of being aggressive and causing venomous bites. It is also non-aggressive which is very fortunate as they are very common on lawns where they create mats of webbing to capture insect prey. And finally, it is an urban myth that the brown recluse spider is present in the Okanagan. This spider is not even present in Canada!

Tick You Off

Female Rocky Mountain wood ticks can cause a condition called tick paralysis in young children (under 10 years old) and pets. From late March to June, female ticks seek blood meals from larger wildlife and livestock. These ticks cling to tall grass and attach to passing victims. It is an urban myth that ticks drop out of trees onto victims. A single adult female tick feeding (sucking blood) on the neck can cause the victim to become paralyzed beginning with the feet and gradually moving upwards over a 5- to 7-day feeding period. Once the tick is properly removed, the victim will make a quick recovery. If not removed, the victim can die from an inability to breathe when the paralysis reaches the chest muscles. Interestingly, the same species located on the Prairies does not cause tick paralysis.

Female Rocky Mountain wood tick

Reports of tick paralysis are rare in the Okanagan. This is due in part to awareness of the threat and people taking precautionary measures to avoid tick attachment (i.e. applying insect repellents). Conducting post-hiking body examinations to locate and remove this little devil also helps.

According to the BC Centre for Disease Control (BCCDC), the BC Interior is also home to the western black-legged tick, less than 1% of which carry the microorganism responsible for causing Lyme disease in people. This tick feeds on the same hosts as the Rocky Mountain wood tick, but it is much rarer in the valley and very unlikely to be encountered by hikers. The BCCDC also reports that there have only been seven cases of the disease confirmed in the Okanagan since 2006. Lyme disease can cause serious, long term disability if left untreated, and its diagnosis, or apparent lack thereof, continues to be controversial across Canada.

Chapter 26

SKIING – FEW LOCATIONS CAN OFFER THIS

There are very few locations in North America which offer the variety of fun and excitement that people can experience while having some form of apparatus attached to their feet. In fact, we can think of no other location where skiing enthusiasts can downhill ski, snowboard, cross-country ski and water-ski . . . all on the same day, if they had a mind to.

Downhill Excitement

Let us begin with downhill skiing and snowboarding which are the highest profile sporting activities that Kelowna is known for on an international scale. There are three ski resorts within a practical drive: Big White (60 min.), Silver Star (70 min.), and Apex (85 min.). Table 1 provides comparative data that should interest all skiing fans. Space limitations prevent us from sharing more comparisons which would further prove that Big White is, indeed, a world class ski resort.

Table 1. Comparison of snow skiing destinations in Western North America.

	Big White, BC	**Silver Star, BC**	**Apex, BC**	**Whistler, BC***	**Whitefish, MT**	**Aspen Mtn, CO**
Ave. Annual Snowfall	750 cm (24.5 ft.)	700 cm (23 ft.)	600 cm (20 ft.)	1022 cm (33.5 ft.)	762 cm (25 ft.)	760 cm (25 ft.)
Summit Elevation	2,319 m (7,606 ft.)	1,915 m (6,280 ft.)	2,180 m (7,200 ft.)	2,436 m (7,160 ft.)	2,078 m (6,817 ft.)	3,417 m (11,212 ft.)
Vertical Drop	777 m (2,550 ft.)	760 m (2,500 ft.)	610 m (2,000 ft.)	1,565 m (5,135 ft.)	717 m (2,353 ft.)	996 m (3,267 ft.)
Number of Lifts	15	11	4	39	14	8
Number of Runs	118	132	67	200	105	76
Longest Run	7.2 km (4.5 mi.)	8 km (5 mi.)	5 km (3 mi.)	11 km (6.8 mi.)	5.3 km (3.3 mi.)	5 km (3 mi.)
Skiable Area	1,147 ha (2,765 ac.)	1,328 ha (3,282 ac.)	450 ha (1,112 ac.)	3,307 ha (8,171 ac.)	1,222 ha (3,020 ac.)	272 ha (673 ac.)
Resort Area	3.052 ha (7,355 ac.)	N/A	N/A	N/A	1,214 ha (3,000 ac.)	N/A
X-country Length	25 km (16 mi.)	105 km (60 mi.)	56 km (35 mi.)	160 km (99.4 mi.)	N/A	N/A
Night Skiing	Yes	Yes	Yes	No	Yes	No

* Includes Blackcombe

If you have any doubt about the awesome experiences people enjoy at Big White, we offer a sampling of their well-deserved awards .

- 2017 Top 5 - Northwest, Newschoolers.com - *Park Poll;*
- 2017 Best Ski-in/Ski-Out Convenience, *The Telegraph;*

- 2017 Certificate of Excellence, *TripAdvisor;*
- 2016 Big White's TELUS Park named one of the best terrain parks in North America, *USA TODAY 10 Best Awards;*
- 2016 #1 Ski Resort in Canada for 'Best Family Resort', 'Best Grooming' and 'Best Snow', Best of Skiing in Canada Awards, *Ski Canada Magazine;*
- 2015 Test Winner: Accommodation offering directly on the slopes and lifts, *Skiresort.info;*
- 2015 Certificate of Excellence, *TripAdvisor;*
- 2015 #1 Ski Resort in Canada for 'Best Powder', Best of Skiing in Canada Awards, *Ski Canada Magazine.*

Nordic (Cross-Country) Skiing

Nordic skiing is well-suited to the area and a very popular way to enjoy the outdoors while getting a great work-out at the same time. There are five Nordic ski club/areas in the region, not including trails offered by downhill ski operators. If that is not enough, there are thousands of acres of Crown land where people can blaze their own trails.

Table 2. Kelowna area Nordic skiing.

	TeleMark Nordic Club: Glenrosa*	**Kelowna Nordic Ski Club: Hwy 33 SE**	**Kelowna Nordic Ski Club: McCulloch Lake**	**Posthill Lake**
Ski Trail Length	50 km	75 km	69 km	40 km
Snowshoe Trail Length	62 km	75 km	70km	N/A

Equipment Rentals	Yes	No	No	No
Travel Time from Kelowna	25 min	20 min	60 min	45 min

*Has Biathlon Range

Water Skiing and Other Water Sports

At the risk of sounding like a tourist guide, it is difficult not to extol the merits of the many opportunities that local lakes provide for energizing summer fun.

One of the most distinguishing factors that makes our area unique for water sports enthusiasts is the variety of lakes within such a short distance.

Firstly, Okanagan Lake is so huge you can travel for hours and even do over-night stays exploring the many beaches along its 270 km (162 mi.) shoreline. The only negative we can say about this lake is that it can get downright mean and dangerous when a wind comes up. While windy weather is rare, it can come quickly and can be dangerous. Having said this, when the weather is polite, you can enjoy Okanagan Lake using any kind of watercraft from stand-up paddleboards, pedal boats, canoes, kayaks and wind surfers, to 9 m - 12 m (30 ft. - 40 ft.) speedboats, cuddies and sailboats.

Secondly, there are numerous smaller mountain lakes within a 20 – 60 minute drive where one can haul their 3m - 4.3m (10 ft.- 14 ft.) fishing boats, kayaks and canoes. Be sure to check the local regulations as some mountain lakes only permit electric motors, or limit engines to less than 10 hp.

Lastly, there are the more intermediate-sized lakes providing a calm, glass-like surface for some fantastic skiing, wakeboarding, and tubing. Duck Lake, Wood Lake and beautiful Kalamalka Lake are three such lakes located only minutes away, and they provide ample opportunity for boaters to try something a little different from Okanagan Lake.

Regardless of which type of 'board' you strap to your feet, or your skill level, Kelowna offers all the venues you will need to test your skills throughout the year.

CHAPTER 27

GREAT GOLF, BUT AT WHAT PRICE?

While we authors clearly understand the seriousness of the game of golf, we thought it appropriate to take a break from the dryness of so many facts and figures by including some sage advice on this most frustrating of sports.

"Golf is an awkward set of bodily contortions designed to produce a graceful result."

– Tommy Armour

"Golf is a game in which you yell 'fore', shoot six and write down five."

– Paul Harvey

"They call it golf because all the other four letter words were taken."

– Ray Floyd

"Golf can best be defined as an endless series of tragedies obscured by the occasional miracle."

– Author Unknown

By The Numbers

Table 1. Descriptions and prices of Kelowna and area golf courses.

Course Name	Max. Slope M/W	Yardage M/W	2018 Rate[1]	Annual Member Fee[2]	Initia-tion Fee
Black Mountain	125/124	6408/4574	$95	$2,999[6]	N/A
Gallagher's Canyon[3]	129/137	6802/5574	$130	$2,389	$3,800
Gallagher's Canyon - Pinnacle (9-hole x 2)	96/107	3968/3968	$54	$995	$0
Harvest Golf Club	127/133	7109/6065	$135	$2,575	$0
Kelowna Golf & Country Club[4]	131/133	6344/4377	$95	See[4]	$7,500
Kelowna Springs[3]	123/118	6256/5225	$92	$1,922	$2,750[7]
Michaelbrook Ranch	84/86	3721/3382	$53	$1,430	$0
Mission Creek	98/97	3873/3307	$47	$1,410	$0
Okanagan GC - The Bear	133/136	6885/5100	$130	$2,799[5]	$0
Okanagan GC - The Quail	138/137	6794/4713	$130	$2,799[5]	$0
Orchard Greens (9-hole x 2)	98/97	2099/1874	$54[7]	$1,100	$0
Predator Ridge - The Predator Course	139/134	7057/5238	$170	$3,600[6]	$35,000
Predator Ridge - The Ridge Course	133/134	7123/5047	$180	$3,600[6]	$35,000
Shadow Ridge Golf Club	124/129	6423/5493	$72	$1,475	$0
Shannon Lake	125/134	6294/5445	$83	$1,949	$15,000[7]
Sunset Ranch	126/130	6500/5055	$89[8]	$1,879	$0
The Rise	137/142	6843/5269	$109	$3,300[6]	$0
Tower Ranch	127/141	7212/5489	$130	$3,300[6]	$0
Two Eagles	114/111	5014/3785	$70	$1,950	N/A

[1]Prime time for 18 holes w/power cart unless otherwise noted; [2]Membership fees are unlimited play not including power cart unless otherwise noted; [3]Semi-Private; [4]Associate dues are $440 & includes 20 rounds at $53 F & B assess of $500; [5]Includes play at both Bear & Quail; [6]Includes power cart; [7]Estimate; [8]Less food voucher.

We realize that both Predator courses, and particularly the Rise course, are all closer to the city of Vernon than they are to Kelowna. Rather than break tradition with most other publications, we decided that given their very close proximity to Kelowna, we would follow suit and include these three amazing courses in our research as well.

Figure 1 is a map showing the locations of the 19 golf courses in Kelowna, West Kelowna and Lake Country.

Figure 1. Location of golf courses in the Kelowna area. Map courtesy Tourism Kelowna.

National Recognition/Awards

1. Four of our courses ranked in The SCORE*Golf* Top 59 Best Public Courses in Canada for 2017.
    - #9 - Predator Ridge - The Ridge Course

- #18 - Tower Ranch
- #24 - Gallagher's Canyon
- #25 - Predator Ridge - The Predator Course

2. One ranking in *The Canadian Golf Magazine Top 50 - 2017*

    - #19 - Predator Ridge - The Predator Course

3. Three of our courses ranked in *The Canadian Golf Magazine Top 50 Best You Can Play 2016.*

    - # 10 - Predator Ridge - The Ridge Course
    - # 37 - Predator Ridge - The Predator Course
    - # 50 - Tower Ranch

What is Unique About our Golf Opportunities?

In keeping with our goal of providing readers with information that is distinctive to our location, we have created a short list of things which highlight our uniqueness.

- *Season Length:* Our season is generally eight months long, which makes this area the envy of many potential newcomers. In fact, this is one of the few places in Canada where you can downhill ski during the morning hours and play a round of golf in the afternoon.
- *Tremendous Array of Elevations:* Golf is not supposed to be a dangerous sport, but taking your eye off some of the cart paths in the higher elevation courses could result in a descent down a rocky mountain-side, marking the end of one's golf season.
- *Truly Unique Setting:* Many of our courses have their fairways lined with fruit trees and/or vineyards.
- *Night Golf*: We do have one 9-hole course which offers night golf. Orchard Greens Golf Course shines bright to 11:00 p.m. This is the only club in the Okanagan to floodlight its course.

- *We Have More Golf Courses Per Capita*: There are an estimated 2,400 golf courses across Canada, and Statistics Canada pegs the number of golfers in Canada at about 1.5 million. That's one course for every 625 players, or 14,500 Canadians, among the highest number per capita in the world. Using this type of analysis, we find that the Kelowna CMA has one course for every 11,240 residents, or more than the average number of golf courses available to residents in Canada.
- *Reasonable Rates:* It appears that the number of local courses creates sufficient competition in order to keep rates and club membership fees in line with, or better than, comparable opportunities across Canada. This suggestion is based solely on feedback from friends and family, along with a few online rate comparisons.
- *Ogopogo Invitational Golf Tournament:* This 65 year-old golf tournament is the largest amateur golf tournament in British Columbia and is held every July at the beautiful Kelowna Golf & Country Club.
- *Umbrella Rarely Needed:* We have been golfing weekly for several years and can honestly say that we have cancelled tee times less than five times. Only one of our foursome carries an umbrella, despite the fact that we should probably all use umbrellas to provide shade.
- *No Mosquitoes:* Well, we may see the odd one, but another check of our foursome revealed that only one of us carries mosquito spray in his bag.

Kelowna offers casual and committed golfers a great variety of golf courses in close proximity. The golfer's only major challenge are pars, not rain and mosquitoes!

CHAPTER 28

A HIKING EXTRAVAGANZA

The topography of the Kelowna area provides a truly unique and interesting experience for hikers and bikers of all description. Where else can one find flat and elevated trails bordering a beautiful long lake, surrounded by orchards and vineyards nestled below and on the sides of forested mountains? This chapter describes the many opportunities to walk, hike or cycle in and around Kelowna, and enjoy the scenery while getting healthful exercise.

The following is a list of local organizations that support and promote hiking in the central Okanagan.

- Central Okanagan Naturalists Club
- Central Okanagan Outdoors Club
- Friends of the South Slopes Society
- HikingAddiction
- Myra Canyon Trestle Restoration Society

The City of Kelowna has developed a website, Active by Nature, to encourage citizens and visitors to get out and explore Kelowna and its beautiful scenery and amenities. The site includes an interactive map that displays the various routes throughout the city and surrounding countryside (Fig. 1). Tourism Kelowna also hosts a web page, Kelowna Hiking Trails, which provides descriptions of 19 trails in the Kelowna area, 10 in Lake Country, and 17 in West Kelowna-Peachland.

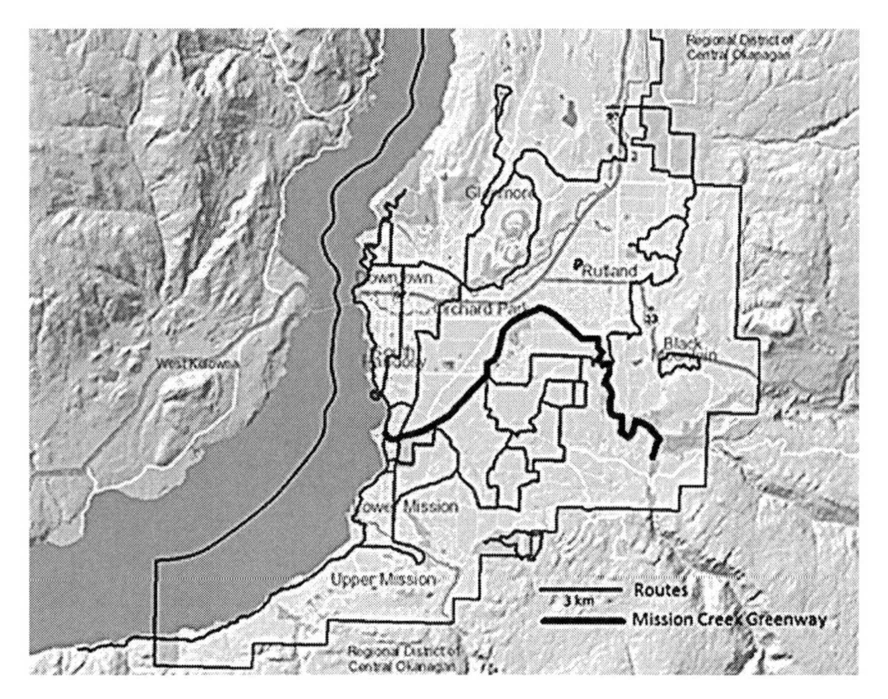

Figure 1. Map showing routes for walking or cycling in and around Kelowna including Mission Creek Greenway. Courtesy City of Kelowna.

For those who want to remain active walkers but find hiking trails a bit too physically challenging, you can enjoy a walk route, as described by one of our more mature friends:

> *...we walk the waterfront often...... from the free parking north of the Bird Sanctuary, past the Dolphins and Sails, to the tunnel under the bridge, and return is 5 KM.... on Sundays we continue from the Bridge to the Hospital via the Abbot walkway..... Far more interesting people watching than the other locations, and elderly people with their new knees and hips like flat, solid pavement...*

Mission Creek Greenway

A very popular year-round trail within Kelowna for walkers, hikers, cyclists and horseback riders is the Mission Creek Greenway (Fig. 1). It follows the tree-lined Mission Creek from Lakeshore Road upstream for 16.5 km (10.3 mi.) to Scenic Canyon Regional Park. Construction began in 2015 to extend the trail about 6 km (3.7 mi.) to Mission Creek Falls where visitors will see more interesting geological formations and scenery. An estimated 1,000 people use the Greenway each day to enjoy the scenery, observe wildlife (including spawning kokanee), socialize or exercise.

It is important to note that if you are hiking near an orchard or vineyard, please do not pick the fruit. You do not know what may have been sprayed on the fruit, and the fruit does not belong to you. Also, abuse of this warning causes growers to oppose hiking trails adjacent to their land.

Myra Canyon Trestles

One of the most popular and world-famous local trails for walking, hiking or cycling is the Myra Canyon Trestles in the Myra-Bellevue Provincial Park (Fig. 2). Trestles, or train bridges, were built to span the many gorges between Myra and Ruth stations. The trail is part of the old Kettle Valley Railway that ceased to operate in 1972. The track bed starts in Midway, BC (SE of Kelowna near the US border) and after Kelowna leads to Penticton, Summerland, Princeton and ends at Hope. Sections of the railway bed have become part of the Trans Canada Trail. In 2003, the Myra Canyon section was designated a National Historic Site.

It takes up to 4.3 hours to walk the 24 km (15 mi.) section between Myra (elev. 1,258 m) and Ruth (elev. 1,274 m). This trek includes 18 wooded or steel trestles which vary in length from 23 to 220 m and in height from 3 to 55 m. You will also travel through two tunnels, 84 and 114 m in length. It is very flat and thus very easy to walk, cycle or push a stroller. All the trestles have been upgraded with sturdy side railings and surface planking.

The Kelowna Daily Courier reported that in 2015, about 59,000 visitors experienced the breath-taking views of Kelowna and Okanagan Lake from these trestles.

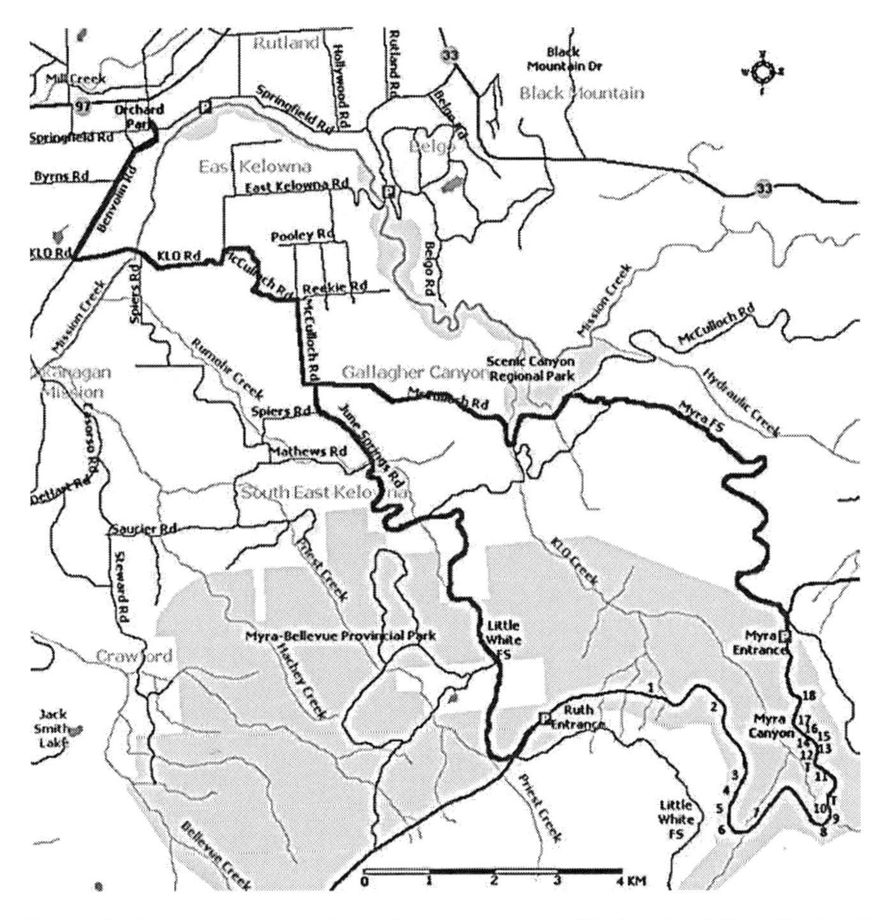

Figure 2. Access routes to Myra Canyon entrances (Ruth, Myra) from Orchard Park Shopping Centre and location of the 18 trestles and two tunnels (T).

Local hikers and cyclists are excited about plans for a new 48.5 km (30 mi.) trail called the Okanagan Rail Trail. It will use the former CNR railway allowance between Kelowna and Vernon. The communities of Vernon, Kelowna and Lake Country jointly purchased the 4.5 m wide right-of-way that follows the shoreline of Wood and Kalamalka lakes for half of its journey to Vernon. Fund-raising efforts are underway to develop the rail bed into a year-round walking/hiking and cycling trail (estimated to cost $160.00/m). According to the *Okanagan Rail Trail Impact Assessment*

Report, the trail will attract an estimated 148,000 walking trips and 309,095 cycling trips per year.

This chapter provides only a very brief introduction to the hiking and cycling opportunities that await you in Kelowna. In fact, describing this chapter as *A Hiking Extravaganza* may have been an understatement.

CHAPTER 29

MINUTES' DRIVE TO TROUT-FILLED LAKES

Fishers all like to dream about catching the BIG ONE. There are about 100 lakes within an hour drive of Kelowna that the avid and occasional fisher can enjoy; the lakes are stocked with rainbow trout and other species (some illegally introduced like perch and carp). There are lakes along valley bottoms (Okanagan, Duck, Wood, Kalamalka lakes) and many lakes up in the hills, some of which are man-made reservoirs created for irrigation districts.

So, where do we start? For sure, one must read the *BC Freshwater Fishing Regulations Synopsis* as there are many regulations that cover all aspects of fishing Interior lakes and streams.

The next question is – how much does a license cost? Table 1 shows the cost of a basic angling license for residents and non-residents. Persons under 16 years of age do not need a license nor be accompanied by an adult with a license, and they can have their own quota of fish.

Table 1. Prices of basic angling licenses, April 1, 2018 to March 31, 2019.

	BC Resident	Canadian Resident	Non-Resident Alien
Annual Angling	$36	$55	$80
One Day Angling[1]	$10	$20	$20
Eight Day Angling[1]	$20	$36	$50
Annual License for Disabled	$1	$55[2]	$80[2]
Annual License for Age 65 Plus	$5	$55	$80

[1]You may buy as many one day and eight day licenses as you need, but only one annual license. [2]Fee reduction not available.

You can purchase your angling license online (www.fishing.gov.bc.ca). You can also buy a freshwater fishing license from one of the many fishing license vendors throughout BC or over the counter at a Service BC office. You must always carry the license with you. We always keep a copy in our tackle box in a sealable plastic bag. You should also keep a copy in your vehicle in case you lose your tackle box in the lake (Heaven forbid!).

But that may not be the only license you need. Transport Canada requires that all persons operating a powered pleasure craft used for recreational purposes in Canada must obtain a lifetime Pleasure Craft Operator Card. You can take a free online course and, after passing the timed online test, pay the $39.95 fee to print off your temporary card to use until your permanent card arrives in the mail.

According to our fishing buddies, the size of boat you need depends on where you plan to do most of your fishing and the number of people who will be fishing with you. For most lakes, boats lengths 3.6 m (12 ft.) or less are fine for 1-3 people. However, if you plan to fish large lakes like Okanagan and Kalamalka, especially well off-shore, you should use at least a 5 m (16 ft.) long boat. As for power, a 3 hp gas or electric motor is sufficient for most upper lakes, but a 9 hp will give you the power you need on all lakes (accept Okanagan Lake), especially under windy conditions. By federal regulations, all boats are required to carry safety equipment. What exactly must be carried depends on the type and size of boat. Transport Canada Marine website has much more detailed information.

Once you have your fishing gear, boat and licenses, you must decide which lake will give you the best opportunity to catch a meal or two, or simply to enjoy the sport (catch and release). The best source of information is of course local fishers, followed by local fishing supplies retailers. The website *Anglers Atlas* offers a free subscription to information about lakes anywhere in the world.

Fishing is best in the spring right after the ice leaves (April-May) and in the early fall (September-October). Upper lakes are accessible off major highways using provincial forestry and logging roads. In some cases, you may have to walk in. Watch for signs indicating loggings trucks are active. Before going to any upper lake it is best to check if a four-wheel vehicle is necessary. A spare battery for your electric motor is essential as many campsites do not have power. Have warm clothing and rain gear along as it can turn wet or cold quickly in the upper lakes. You will be lucky to have cell phone reception, but then why ruin your trip?

Camping and boat launch facilities can vary greatly depending on whether privately or government owned. Check the BC government recreation Sites and Trails BC/Okanagan District website which lists facilities, services, uses and access for 129 BC Forest Service recreation sites in the Okanagan. Some lakes have pretty tight or steep boat launches so make sure that your trailer backing skills are honed up. Please remember to always take out what you bring in. Fire pits and cut wood may or may not be provided.

A favourite local fishing resort is the Chute Lake resort. It has a licensed lodge (8 rooms), variously serviced cabins (8) and campsites (36) located beside the historic Kettle Valley Railway. It's only about a half hour drive up from Okanagan Mission. Watercraft are available for rent along with a boat launch.

Okanagan Lake is home to rainbow, brook and lake trout, kokanee (land-locked salmon), carp, whitefish, perch, burbot and bass. Many fishers report great success capturing rainbow trout by trolling lures, especially Apex lures. Rainbow trout can reach 9 kg (20 lbs.); lake whitefish and burbot also reach sizes that will make you proud.

There are very few rivers and streams to fish in the Okanagan, but you can fish the creek mouths in the spring with light tackle.

Kokanee is another favourite sport fish, but numbers are still trying to recover from devastating losses after the introduction of Mysis shrimp in 1966. Mysis were introduced to provide an additional food source for rainbow trout and enhance the fishery. Unfortunately these shrimp competed with young kokanee for the same food source (phytoplankton). Today kokanee are making a recovery, in part due to the unique Okanagan Lake Mysis Fishery. You might notice some large fishing vessels on this lake between May and October, especially towards the north end of the lake. They are harvesting Mysis shrimp. The fishery has harvested 657 metric tonnes (723 tons) of shrimp which is processed into fish food.

Well, it's time to reel in and point the bow to shore. We hope this brief introduction to sport fishing in the Kelowna area will encourage you and your family to try your luck and enjoy the great outdoors.

CHAPTER 30

MINOR SPORTS ORGANIZATIONS

Kelowna is fortunate to have many minor sports organizations for all age groups and athletic abilities. Just as important is the fact that we have many people who are willing to volunteer their time and talent to support teams in activities ranging from coaching to fundraising. Kelowna also has a very supportive business community who sponsor teams and events which really help to make the organizations thrive.

In this chapter we will introduce you to the scope of the minor sport organizations and to the indoor and outdoor facilities available for use throughout the year.

Table 1 lists the name and use of the sports fields corresponding to the map numbers.

Figure 1 shows the location of sports fields in Kelowna. Many are part of parks that also have washrooms, playgrounds, trails and other amenities. Check for more details about each field on the City of Kelowna Parks & Recreation/Sports Fields website.

Table 1. Sports fields in Kelowna and sports activities.

Map #	Sports Field/Park	Sports
1	High Noon Park	Softball
2	Glenmore Sports Park	Softball
3	Edith Gay Park	Baseball, pickleball, tennis
4	Rutland Recreation Park	Baseball, BMX, soccer
5	Belgo Park	Softball
6	Summerside Park	Soccer, softball, tennis
7	South Kelowna Centennial Park	Multi-courts, soccer, softball
8	East Kelowna Park	Softball
9	Johnson Park	Soccer
10	Dilworth Soccer Park	Soccer
11	Lillooet Park	Multi-courts, soccer
12	Jack Robertson Memorial Park	Softball, tennis
13	Recreation Avenue Park	Baseball, curling
14	Martin Park	Soccer
15	City Park	Basketball, lawn bowling, multi-court, sand volleyball, soccer, swimming, tennis
16	Parkinson Recreation Park	Cricket, multi-court, pickleball, soccer, tennis
17	Cameron Park	Softball
18	Osprey Park	Baseball
19	KLO Sports Field	Soccer
20	Mission Recreation Park	Softball, soccer (indoor & outdoor)
21	Redridge Park	Soccer
22	Quarry Park	Baseball, soccer
23	Kettle Valley Sports Field	Soccer

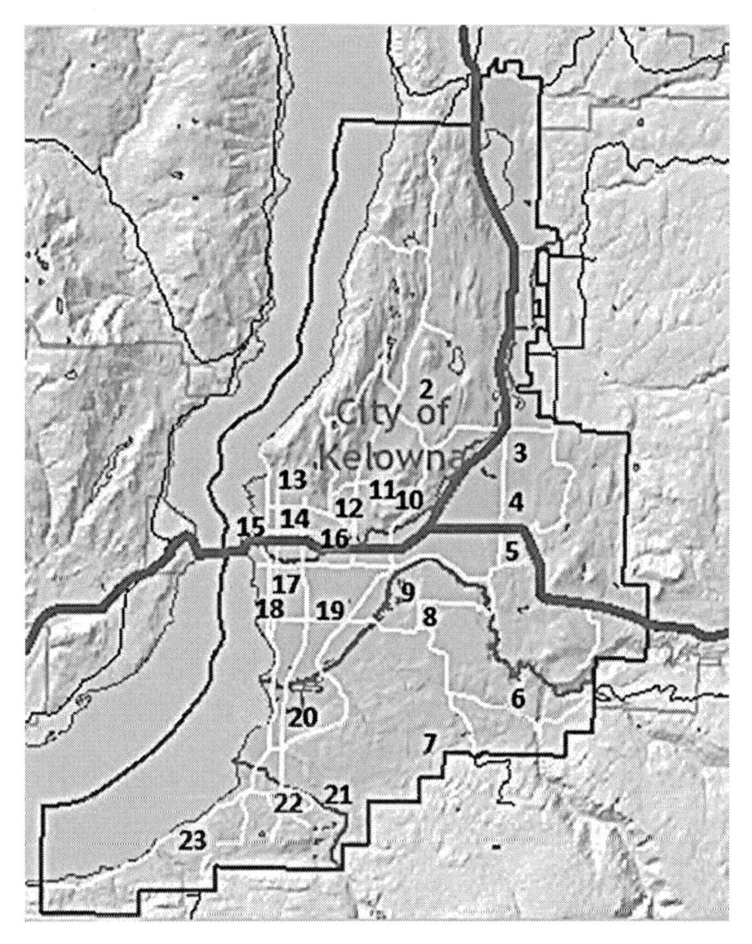

Figure 1. Numbered locations of sports fields in Kelowna.

Recreation Avenue Park (#13) contains our 12-sheet curling rink (tied with Regina and Red Deer for the largest in the world), and four ball fields including King (fastball), Elks (baseball), and Lions Park (baseball). Teams from the Kelowna Curling Club have won numerous Canadian and world championships as well as the 2006 Paralympics Wheelchair Curling Gold Medal.

There are a number of private sports facilities where members can play various indoor sports recreationally or competitively. Examples include badminton, floor hockey, martial arts, handball, squash, racquetball, volleyball, and dodge ball.

Kelowna has many community minor sports organizations, some affiliated with provincial governing bodies, providing organized sporting activities and events throughout the year. Table 3 includes a list of the sports organizations active in Kelowna.

Table 3. List of non-profit sports organizations in Kelowna.

Kelowna Non-Profit Sports Organizations	
BC Mainland Cricket League	Kelowna Minor Football
Central Okanagan Outdoors Club	Kelowna Minor Hockey Association
Central Okanagan Rugby Enthusiasts	Kelowna Minor Lacrosse
Central Okanagan Sailing Association	Kelowna Nordic Cross Country Ski Club
Central Okanagan Youth Soccer	Kelowna Ringette Association
Kelowna Aquajets Swim Club	Kelowna Skating Club
Kelowna Area Cycling Coalition	Kelowna Springboard Diving Club
Kelowna Lawn Bowling Club	Pickleball Kelowna
Kelowna Adult Softball Association	Okanagan Athletics Club
Kelowna and District Fish & Game Club	Okanagan Club for Skiing, Sports & Socials
Kelowna Badminton Club	Okanagan Hockey Group
Kelowna BMX Club	Okanagan Masters Swim Club
Kelowna Canoe and Kayak Club	Okanagan Mission Tennis Club
Kelowna Curling Club	Old-Timers Hockey
Kelowna Junior Racquetball	Orchard City Hockey League
Kelowna Major Men's Fastball	Vancouver Family Tae Kwan Do Society
Kelowna Master's Racquetball	Vancouver Minor Baseball
Kelowna Minor Baseball	Stick Fix Kelowna - Hockey Stick Fix

The 13-league Kelowna Minor Hockey Association organizes the annual 5-day BDO Kelowna International Elite Midget Tournament where top midget teams compete from across Canada and the US.

We are also proud of our junior semi-pro sports teams that represent Kelowna in some national and international sports leagues:

- The Kelowna Falcons Baseball Club, one of two Canadian teams in the West Coast League (BC and Western US), playing out of Elks Stadium.
- The Okanagan Sun, a very successful football team in the BC Junior Football League, playing out of the Apple Bowl stadium.
- The Kelowna Rockets Junior A hockey team, another very victorious sports team in the Western Hockey League that plays out of Prospera Place hockey arena.

As you can see, Kelowna has the organizational infrastructure and facilities to meet the sporting needs of almost everyone. We are especially grateful for the local volunteers without whom organized minor sports would not exist.

CHAPTER 31

CULTURAL ACTIVITIES

Providing an assessment of how culturally vibrant a community might be is no simple task. Firstly, there are varied definitions of the non-biological meaning of the word "culture". Secondly, the cultural aspects of a city are often quite subjective in nature which makes it challenging to provide a meaningful comparison to other communities. Culture must be "lived in" to be fully understood and appreciated.

When people are trying to determine if a new community is culturally active, they may ask questions like how many museums does it have, how many art galleries does it have and, above all, does it have its own symphony? If these are the cornerstones of a healthy cultural scene, then Kelowna fairs well in that it is host to three public museums, two public art galleries, two performing arts theatres, and the third largest professional symphony orchestra in British Columbia.

More specifically, Kelowna is home to the following cultural facilities:

- Alternator Centre for Contemporary Arts
- Artwalk
- Father Pandosy Mission
- Kasugai Gardens
- Laurel Packing House
- Kelowna Community Theatre (including the Black Box Theatre)
- Kelowna Art Gallery

- Kelowna Actors Studio
- Okanagan Heritage Museum
- Okanagan Wine and Orchard Museum
- Okanagan Military Museum
- Okanagan Regional Library
- Rotary Centre for the Arts & the Mary Irwin Theatre
- Festivals Kelowna

The map below illustrates a self-guided walking tour of the downtown cultural district of Kelowna. To take a virtual walk, visit Kelowna.ca and download their free app.

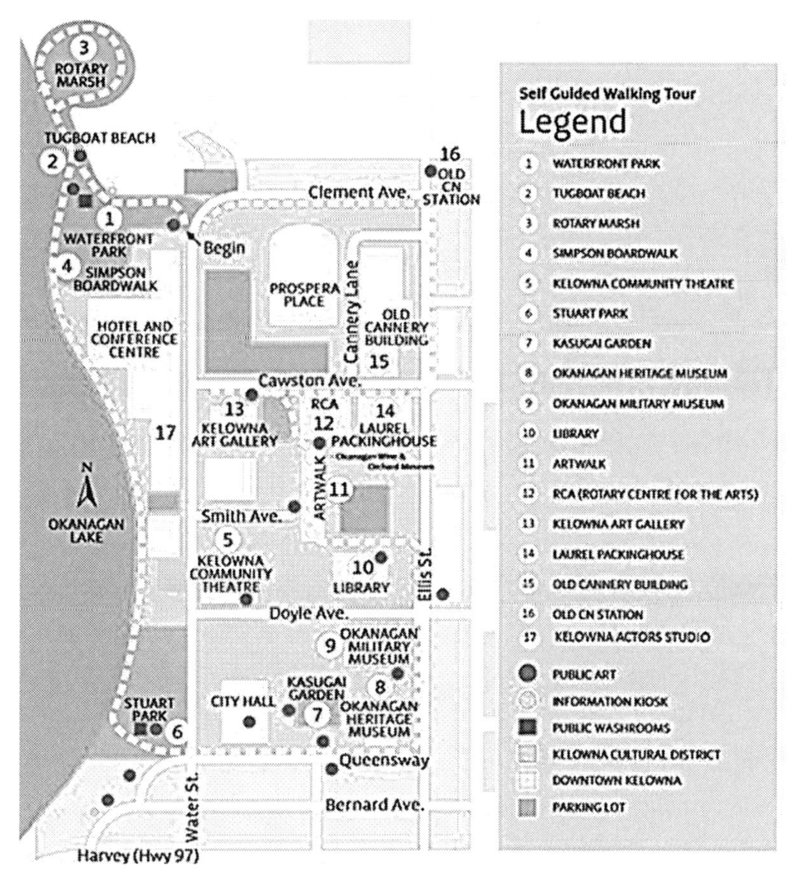

Figure 1. Cultural District of Kelowna (Map courtesy City of Kelowna).

Opera Kelowna Society

The Opera Kelowna Society website states that it is a registered non-profit regional opera company and training centre for young promising classical artists in the Okanagan Valley. The performing season is focused on one full main stage opera each year, with several operatic productions to round out the season. The Society offers Young Artist Vocal Education and outreach programs – In-Class Opera Productions and School Tours – introducing opera to schools and engaging youth in our community in the cultural experience that is opera.

Okanagan Symphony Orchestra (OSO)

The Okanagan Symphony Orchestra began modestly as a small group of enthusiasts meeting in Penticton in the fall of 1959. Now in its 57th year, the orchestra has developed from a largely amateur organization, with a part-time manager and a part-time conductor, to an excellent regional orchestra with a full-time executive director, a full-time music director, a core of 20 professional musicians, plus support staff. The OSO also has access to dozens of professional and non-professional musicians, as needs dictate. The OSO office is in Kelowna and performances are held here as well as Vernon and Penticton.

Okanagan Symphony Youth Orchestra (OSYO)

Founded by world-renowned composer Imant Raminsh, the OSYO was formed to promote the importance of music education at the highest level, especially to our youth. Over the last few years, under the directorship of Rosemary Thomson and Dennis Colpitts, the OSYO has grown considerably showing the clear need and desire to engage youth in making live music together. Their shared passion for music education is contagious among these young musicians – many of whom decide to pursue promising musical careers.

Kelowna Actors Studio (KAS)

According to their promotional material, KAS is the Okanagan's only licensed dinner theatre and performing arts school. It was formed in 2003 to: produce exciting presentations of the world's best-loved Broadway productions; present enriching learning experiences for students; become the premiere forerunner and prime example of a high-quality theatre company; and to enrich the cultural landscape of the Okanagan Valley.

The KAS offers approximately 1,021 m^2 (11,000 $ft.^2$) of space. It houses a 230-seat theatre including 91 dinner seats with full table service, a mirrored rehearsal/dance studio, set and props construction/storage, kitchen, licensed bar and a general office area.

Rotary Centre for the Arts & the Mary Irwin Theatre

This facility is a multi-purpose centre that hosts visual and performing arts events (concerts, art exhibits, lectures) and activities (dance, music, pottery, kid's camps, and more) for all age groups.

Festivals Kelowna

Festivals Kelowna is a non-profit society that produces free outdoor programs and events including Parks Alive, the Kelowna Buskers Program, Arts on the Avenue, the Celebrate Canada Day – Kelowna festivities, and New York New Year's Eve family celebration. It also presents Buskers on Bernard in mid-August, a showcase of its Kelowna Buskers Program.

Significant Municipal Support for Culture

The approved provisional 2018 city budget shows that cultural services and facilities are allocated \$3.66 million or 2.8% of the total net operating budget of \$131.66 million. On a per capita basis this represents approximately \$28 per person (population of 129,500 in 2017).

From a personal perspective, we have noticed a very positive change in cultural initiatives over the last ten years or so. A couple of examples that come to mind are the increase in the number of available live theatre performances, and the huge increase in the number of pieces of outdoor public art, which now stands at 60.

It was during our research for this chapter that we discovered why the last few years have seen such a tangible enrichment to the local cultural scene. First, the City of Kelowna created a Cultural Services Department led by a dedicated fulltime staff complement. Second, they sanctioned the *2012-2017 Cultural Services Plan*. We encourage readers to take a look at this plan available at kelowna.ca. It is extremely well done and includes specific goals and detailed strategies to achieve them.

With the people and plan now in place, the City of Kelowna has set out to make real and positive change for the community. As stated earlier, our opinion is that they have been successful in doing this and commend those responsible for the development and implementation of our Cultural Services Plan. It proves that our municipal government takes cultural development quite seriously.

See Chapter 40 for our trusted business contact offering a discount on piano tuning services.

CHAPTER 32

NIGHTLIFE

Tourism Kelowna states that Kelowna has over 30 nightlife options available: live music, DJs, comedy, casinos, theatre, dance clubs and karaoke. The night scene in Kelowna is a thriving mix of ultra-hip discos, laid-back lounges, friendly neighbourhood pubs, sports bars, and energetic live theatre and music venues.

Nightlife can mean many different things to many different people, depending upon their age and interests. The reality is that when people ask about nightlife they are generally referring to places where they can go to meet people of the opposite or same sex and be served alcohol. There is no shortage of such establishments in Kelowna, particularly in the downtown core.

As with most cities, our downtown core is where you will find the majority of the action after the sun goes down. For example, all of our four nightclubs are downtown and within walking distance of one another. Our largest casino is downtown, as is our largest single entertainment venue – Prospera Place - a multi-purpose arena with a maximum capacity of 8,000 for concerts.

For a more experienced and sophisticated view of Kelowna's nightlife, we reached out to local professional jazz singer, Anna Jacyszyn, for her own personal interpretation.

> *Nightlife in Kelowna has its own heartbeat. As a person who teeters the seesaw of a young at heart 50 year-old, I still have the instinct to put my hands in the air and wave them like I just don't*

care, to a house beat youth rave party. But then I would have to go to a night club and be served vodka from a gun and wander around feeling like I am patrolling the parameters for underage youth, instead of letting go and submitting to my inner party girl.

For someone like me, who would love to go dancing in an environment of like-minded music lovers, disco, ball-room, boogie-woogie, or just free-stylin' - Kelowna is still an untapped market. The thing is, everyone wants it, but when someone puts in the time, effort and finances to create it, no one wants to pay for it and so it dwindles away.

There are plenty of restaurants in town where sporty casuals or jeans are acceptable. Not one venue insists on a dress code, which defines the mood and vibe of Kelowna. High-end fine dining closes down and goes out of business, and another restaurant serving burgers, pasta, or Caesar salad opens up in its place. There are some wonderful fresh farm to table places to eat and that trend is slowly becoming the norm, but again the menu does not stray from the form of the aforementioned, it's just better ingredients and a higher price.

Most restaurants are dead after 8:00 pm or, if you do choose to dine after that time, the places are so loud with overhead music that you can't socialize with your party.

Many charities hold their annual fundraising Galas which allow people like me to eat, drink, dance and wear a sophisticated frock, but these are usually held at the same ballroom in the same hotel, just a different charity.

There is a lot to choose from when going out in Kelowna. Theatre, Symphony, Opera, Jazz, Blues, Karaoke, and even Country. The talent is very good; even the live music in restaurants and bars tends to be above average. I recommend doing that when choosing your night out.

Anna Jacyszyn has received a number of awards for her achievements in raising the bar for jazz entertainment in Kelowna. She is the founder and host of Jazz Cafe, which is now a nomadic destination for pop-up concerts. In addition to being a freelance reviewer, Anna writes a weekly arts column for the Kelowna Daily Courier, under the name ArtaFact.

CHAPTER 33

RETIREMENT SERVICES

A comfortable retirement is what many of us work towards while trying to successfully raise a family and/or achieve career or business aspirations. The degree of comfort we can expect in our retirement is influenced by our family relationships, health, retirement income, and anticipated life-style. Kelowna is a popular retirement destination, especially for Prairie retirees, because of the milder weather and physical amenities the city and area have to offer. The question is: compared to other cities, what amenities or services does Kelowna offer that makes it an attractive retirement destination?

We have described the many local recreational activities and health care services available in other chapters. This chapter will focus on the amenities that may help to maintain or improve the quality of your retirement living in Kelowna.

Overcoming Retirement Challenges

We begin with Table 1 which lists the various organizations that provide information on many aspects of retirement living. The chapter on Health Care provides information on health care services for seniors. The chapter on Minor Sports Organizations lists facilities for indoor and outdoor sporting activities that include programs for seniors.

Table 1. Organizations delivering educational, recreational and social activities to seniors in Kelowna.

Organization	Services
Seniors Outreach & Resource Centre	A society providing information on resources and services available to seniors, including but not limited to: housing, financial, social, recreational, health, safety, legal and estate-planning. Maintains an online directory of community services for seniors (Elderguide).
Parkinson Senior Society	Dedicated to connecting people 50+ who enjoy an active lifestyle.
Senior Citizens Association of BC, Branch 17	Drop-in centre that provides social and recreational activities - exercise and dance programs, crafts, cards, games and bingo.
Kelowna Community Services	Provides individuals with access to support programs to encourage self-reliance and independence.
Rutland Seniors Society	Organizes a wide variety of recreation and cultural programs for persons 50 years+ (e.g. quilting, dancing, card games, fitness, bingo, badminton).
Society for Learning in Retirement	Provides joint learning opportunities for 50+ retired and semi-retired persons through presentations and courses delivered by peer teachers.

Housing Opportunities

If you plan to own rather than rent, Kelowna offers the same options as most cities, from single to semi-detached to multi-unit residential housing. Kelowna is one of the highest priced housing markets in Canada, as described in Chapter 13 on real estate. Retirees also have the option to buy a home in an adult-oriented or retirement community

(45-55+), some of which are strata developments that have associated monthly maintenance fees.

At some point seniors may need to modify their home in order to accommodate mobility or health issues. BC Housing, a crown corporation, provides financial assistance through its Home Adaptations For Independence (HAFI) program. The program grants up to $20,000 to help eligible low-income individuals to continue living in their homes.

As of the end of 2017, Kelowna's overall rental vacancy rate was essentially zero (0.2%), one of the lowest in Canada. This is unfortunate news for would-be renters. The rental situation for seniors worsened in 2017 according to the CMHC's 2017 Senior's Housing Survey. The survey revealed that the overall vacancy rate for independent living units (bachelor to 3-bedroom) in the Kelowna CMA dropped from 8.0% in 2016 to 4.1%. This figure is just below the provincial average of 4.5%.

Rental housing is available for independent retirees which provides varying levels of supportive, assisted or complex/residential care (24-hour) services. The costs of these services are included in the rent or on a fee-for-service basis (private pay). Before going further, let us clarify what defines the various retiree housing options.

Independent eligible retirees have access to low-income (subsidized) housing administered by a building/housing society or through Interior Health Home and Community Care. No support services are provided by building/housing societies, but some units are designed to accommodate seniors. Interior Health processes applications for those seeking low-income, assisted-living housing.

BC Housing has a program that will be of interest to low-income seniors planning to rent in Kelowna. *The Shelter Aid For Elderly Renters* (SAFER) program provides monthly cash payments to help make rents affordable for BC seniors 60 or over with low to moderate incomes. The maximum gross monthly income is $2,223 for singles and $2,750 for couples. You must have lived in BC for the full 12 months prior to making an application, and spend more than 30% of your gross household income on rent, including pad rent for a manufactured home. There are additional eligibility requirements posted on BC Housing's website.

Our review of posted listings that provide senior housing in Kelowna revealed there are 15 places for low-income retirees, 22 places providing supportive services, 10 assisted-living places, and 10 residential/complex care facilities. There are facilities that offer a variety of care and service levels (campus of care residences) which allow residents to remain in one location as their health needs change.

We reviewed the extensive data published in the CHMC's provincial/regional *2017 Senior's Housing Survey* reports, to compare the rental rates of independent living spaces (including assisted-living) across Canada (Table 2). The data does not include non-market (subsidized) units, respite units, or units where an extra charge is required for complex-care.

Table 2. Average rent ($) of independent living spaces by unit type.

City	Bachelor/ Studio	One Bedroom	Two Bedroom
Victoria	2,266	3,438	4,739
Vancouver	2,220	4,149	6,253
Kelowna	**1,984**	**2,605**	**3,734**
Calgary	2,873	3,868	4,680
Edmonton	2,052	2,742	3,557
Regina	3,233	3,657	4,316
Saskatoon	2,677	2,725	3,146
Winnipeg	2,120	2,597	3,154
Toronto	3,325	4,746	6,331
Ottawa	3,469	4,664	5,608
Montreal	1,369	1,677	2,269
Quebec	1,324	1,752	2,187
Nova Scotia	2,864	3,291	2,844
Newfoundland-Labrador	2,455	2589	No data

Source: CMHC 2017 Senior's Housing Survey.

Kelowna offers a wide range of single and multi-residential facilities that provide varying levels of daily-living support services to allow retirees to live comfortably and safely.

CHAPTER 34

'SURVEY SAYS' – KELOWNA SPEAKS

Every few years our municipal leaders produce a report called the *City of Kelowna Citizen Survey* to gauge public satisfaction with municipal programs and services and to gain insight into citizens' service priorities. The latest survey was done in September 2017 by the market research firm, Ipsos. Results of this survey showed that:

- **95%** of residents surveyed said their quality of life in Kelowna is good or very good.
- Overall **90%** of residents said they are satisfied with the level and quality of services the City of Kelowna provides.
- **84%** of residents said they receive good value for their tax dollars.
- **90%** said their city was safe.

The survey also revealed that residents' top five priorities for investment are:

- Encouraging a diverse supply of housing at different price points
- Traffic flow management
- Drinking water
- Police services
- Fire services

The 2017 Citizen Survey report is posted on the City of Kelowna website www.kelowna.ca.

Starting in 2016, the City initiated a process called Imagine Kelowna to document what citizens loved about Kelowna, what opportunities existed, and proposed solutions to the challenges the city will face going forward. The results listed below are from the first consultative phase involving feedback from 4,000 online and face-to-face interactions with residents, businesses, community leaders, academia, and subject experts.

What citizens love about Kelowna:

- The natural beauty of the area and what it offers (mountains, lake, beaches)
- Recreational activities
- Sense of community

Current challenges facing the community:

- Affordability and housing
- Employment opportunities and wages
- Transportation
- Regional context and sometimes conflicting priorities

Hopes and aspirations for the future Kelowna:

- A healthy density
- Affordability and housing
- A continued sense of community

Opportunities and Strengths:

- City of experiences thanks to the climate and four seasons
- Okanagan Lake and recreational opportunities
- Access to local colleges and world-class university

- Entrepreneurial city
- A community of collaborators

Respondents indicated that managing population growth, transportation planning, and economic opportunities should not adversely impact the feeling of community that citizens value. Environment and traffic safety were also important themes. The draft final report of this 4-phase public consultation initiative is to be presented to City Council in early 2018. More information on this project is available online at imagine.kelowna.ca.

While the above information may be important for city planners to identify the future wants and needs of residents, it doesn't provide much insight into the minds of Kelownians beyond local infrastructure development. In order to provide a deeper understanding of how Kelowna residents feel about important issues, we approached a local news agency for permission to reproduce some of their historical survey results. Castanet.net regularly polls their audience on a wide range of timely topics which are often suggested by the readers themselves. The results of these polls should give potential newcomers a better sense of who we are as people, and as a community in which they might live.

Please note that no one is suggesting these results are statistically valid. They may or may not be. The point is that some information is better than none for those interested in what Kelownians think about important issues. If you want to follow what some Kelownians think about topical issues or to check out survey results not listed below, refer to *Question of the Day* at Castanet.net.

January 2, 2018 (4125 votes) **Should BC Pharmacare cover free abortion pills?**				
Definitely	2121	(51%)	Only some cases	819
Not at all	1020		Undecided	165

October 23, 2017 (5236 votes) **Should school kids be taught about gender equality?**				
Yes	1708		Undecided	440
No	3088	(59%)		

September 28, 2017 (7426 votes) **How would you rate driving through Kelowna on Highway 97?**				
Fine	143	Could be better	1310	
OK	242	Terrible	5731	(77%)

September 27, 2017 (4049 votes) **Is violent crime getting worse in the Okanagan?**				
No	431	Yes	3338	(82%)
Undecided	280			

September 26, 2017 (3404 votes) **Should Crown corporations be privatized?**				
Yes	1564	(45%)	Some of them	970
No	742		Undecided	124

July 19, 2017 (11,639 votes) **Are you in favour of supervised drug consumption sites?**				
No	3555	Yes	4799	(41%)
Undecided	3285			

June 7, 2017 (7173 votes) **Should Canada increase its military spending?**				
Yes	2953	Decrease	3461	(48%)
Leave the same	522	Undecided	207	

April 20, 2017 (8229 votes) **Are you in favour of marijuana legalization?**				
Yes	4029	(49%)	Undecided	324
No	3322		Don't care	554

March 29, 2017 (4327 votes) **Do you support culling city habituated deer?**				
Yes	2415	(56%)		
No	1912			

March 14, 2017 (4014 votes) **How should the city deal with the homeless?**				
Shelter beds	844	Higher welfare	177	
Skills training	941	Crack down	2052	(51%)

February 8, 2017 (5518 votes) **What should be the top priority for Okanagan politicians?**				
Homelessness	683	Economy	1674	(30%)
Housing	1395	Transportation	516	
Public safety	561	Other	222	
Drinking water	467			

September 28, 2016 (10,621 votes) **Should Kelowna follow other communities and ban pit bulls?**				
Yes	3988	No	6633	(63%)

December 22, 2015 (4402 votes) **Your choice of holiday greeting?**				
Merry Christmas	4021	(91%)	Season's greetings	37
Happy holidays	236		Don't celebrate	108

October 7, 2015 (1442 votes) **Do you let your children walk to school?**				
On their own	473	(33%)	They ride the bus	229
In a group	207		Parent drives them	393
With an adult	140			

September 9, 2015 (3246 votes) **Should BC do more to address aboriginal reconciliation?**				
Yes	742	No	2504	(77%)

August 11, 2015 (4102 votes) **Is Kelowna homophobic?**				
Yes	1673	(40%)	Not sure	771
No	1658			

Well, there you have it! Thousands upon thousands of opinions from your future potential neighbours. We would like to add that while these questions may be contentious, varied opinions make life interesting, and our ability to be open-minded, tolerant, and accepting is what makes us Canadian.

CHAPTER 35

OUR TOP 20 ACTIVITIES THAT YOU'LL NEVER GET TIRED OF DOING

All cities have distinct scenic attributes, but some, definitely more than others. Kelowna is clearly in the 'some' category. The local climate supports the growth of a great variety of plants and trees which creates opportunity for amazing scenery. Add water, four seasons, a valley and a few mountains . . . and dare we say . . . 'voilà' . . . near perfection!

If the preceding sounds a little biased, we refer you to a poll taken in February, 2017 by an independent third party that supports our prejudiced claim. Carrentals.com is an Expedia, Inc. Company who created a list of the ***33 Most Scenic Towns in North America.*** Kelowna was included in this list along with: Santa Cruz, CA; Lunenburg, NS; Lake George, NY; Banff, AB; San Juan, PRI; Paia, HI; Quebec City, QC; Lexington, KY.

The following list describes 20 of the many venues that we believe you will never tire of experiencing.

- ***Myra-Bellevue Provincial Park***: Contains the scenic Myra Canyon and the abandoned Kettle Valley Railway with its 18 trestles and two tunnels.

- ***Big White Ski Resort***: It's all about the snow. An average of 7.62 m (25 ft.) of the finest, dry, champagne powder falls annually. Third largest resort in BC with the largest night skiing area in Western Canada.
- ***Mission Creek Park:*** Includes the 12 km (7.5 mi.) long Mission Creek Greenway walking trail.
- ***Cultural District:*** The downtown area abounds with galleries, theatres, museums, and our own professional symphony.
- ***Winery Tours & Festivals:*** Local wineries are forever changing their offerings to attract and wow residents and visitors alike. Add in a spring and fall wine festival, and you'll be ready to plan a new wine list.
- ***Nine Sandy Beaches:*** Truly awesome clean, sandy swimming beaches, including many amenities and attractions.
- ***Knox Mountain:*** Drive or hike up to the top lookout for a panoramic view of Kelowna and Okanagan Lake.
- ***H20 Adventure and Fitness Centre:*** The largest municipal water park in Canada with an Olympic length pool, wave pool, river run, water slides, a kid's spray park and a surf wave simulator. Also includes 12,000 $ft.^2$ of fitness and cardio space.
- ***Okanagan Mountain Provincial Park:*** Above Okanagan Lake, over 10,000 hectares of rugged landscape with mountain lakes, grasslands and spruce-fir forests. The 33 km (20.5 mi.) shoreline has six marine campgrounds among secluded bays and beaches.
- ***Father Pandosy Mission:*** Restored buildings of the Mission established by Father Pandosy in 1859.
- ***Kasugai Gardens:*** This downtown park integrates traditional elements notable in Japanese gardens, such as stone lanterns, pine trees, waterfalls and a pond stocked with Koi.

- ***The Laurel Packinghouse:*** This 104 year-old former packing house is home to the Okanagan Wine Industry Museum and the British Columbia Orchard Industry Museum.
- ***Parks Alive:*** A summer long community-oriented weekly program offering free live performances of music and other cultural activities.
- ***Kelowna Farmers and Crafters Market:*** An outdoor market featuring products from local area farm, food and craft vendors.
- ***19 Area Golf Courses:*** A wide variety of well-maintained local golf courses for all skill levels, most with beautiful views of the mountains or lake.
- ***Capital News Centre***: This recreation complex has two indoor artificial turf fields, two NHL-sized rink surfaces, an indoor running track, athlete development centre and physiotherapy clinic, meeting rooms, fully-licensed restaurant, and a branch of the Okanagan Regional Library.
- ***Fat Cat Children's Festival:*** An annual festival held in June, this event explores some of the stories and history of the Central Okanagan as part of a high-calibre children's entertainment and learning experience.
- ***Guisachan Heritage Park:*** These historic perennial gardens are open for tours and special events.
- ***Kelowna Art Gallery:*** Produces exhibitions of both historical and contemporary Canadian art. Also offers art classes, workshops and special events.
- ***Prospera Place:*** Home to our WHL Kelowna Rockets hockey club, it can handle 6,500 hockey fans and up to 8,000 concert-goers. Conveniently located right downtown, it is the largest single venue in the Okanagan.

Choosing only twenty top things to see and do was a difficult proposition. There are many additional beautiful and interesting places to visit in the area. We have listed venues that are relatively unique and have a permanence that newcomers can enjoy over a lifetime.

PART THREE

The Economy

"IF ALL THE ECONOMISTS WERE LAID END TO END, THEY'D NEVER REACH A CONCLUSION."
GEORGE BERNARD SHAW

CHAPTER 36

KEY INDUSTRIES – THERE'S A NEW KID ON THE BLOCK

The most common and accurate way to identify key industries in a market area is to measure the economic output of each industry, in dollar terms. Generally, this economic activity is termed Gross Domestic Product (GDP) of a given market area. While such data is readily available on a national and provincial level, it is rarely available at the municipal level, without undertaking specialized and costly studies.

Most sub-provincial markets use the number of people employed in a given industry to gain an understanding of the importance of that industry, relative to others, and to the local economy as a whole.

Table 1 lists the key industries in the Kelowna CMA according to employment levels during the week May 1-7, 2016. The Service Producing Industries employed 79% of the work force compared to 21% for the Goods Producing Industries. According to the 2017 Central Okanagan Economic Development Commission, the Central Okanagan experienced a 29% increase in job postings in 2017, with an average of 1,298 jobs posted per month. The top three categories included – Sales and Service Occupations (32.4%), Trades, Transport & Equipment Operator Occupations (9.9%) and Business, Finance and Administration Occupations (9.9%).

Table 1. Distribution of the employed labour force aged 15 years and over by industry sectors, Kelowna CMA, 2016

Industrial Sector	(000's)	% of Total
Total Employed, All Industries	102.3	100.0
Goods Producing Sectors	21.2	20.7
Agriculture, forestry, fishing, mining and hunting	2.2	2.1
Mining, quarrying, and oil & gas extraction	1.6	1.6
Utilities	0.5	0.5
Construction	11.1	10.9
Manufacturing	5.8	5.6
Services Producing Sector	80.9	79.3
Wholesale trade	3.0	3.0
Retail trade	13.3	13.0
Transportation & warehousing	4.2	4.1
Finance, insurance, real estate, rental and leasing	5.8	5.6
Professional, scientific and technical services	6.8	6.7
Business & waste management, administrative, support, and remediation services	5.2	5.1
Educational services	6.3	6.2
Health care and social assistance	13.4	13.1
Information and cultural industries	2.1	2.0
Arts, entertainment and recreation	2.6	2.5
Accommodation and food services	9.6	9.4
Other services (except public administration)	5.0	4.9
Public administration	3.6	3.5

Source: Statistics Canada 2016 Census of Population, Statistics Canada Catalogue No. 98-400-X2016290.

The New Kid on the Block

Kelowna is often touted as the newest technology hub in BC. Further, it is regularly suggested that technology is becoming one of our largest industries.

When it comes to local technology support and development, Accelerate Okanagan (AO) is where the action is. AO helps tech companies start and grow in the Okanagan by providing expert guidance from ten employed staff, six "executives in residence" and an eleven-member Board of Directors. It is funded federally through the National Research Council (NRC), and provincially through BC Innovation Council (BCIC). As such, AO is a not-for-profit, zero-equity-stake association model.

Our primary source of information on the topic of technology is from the *Economic Impact of the Okanagan Tech Sector: 2015 Edition,* prepared for Accelerate Okanagan by Small Business BC, released September 2016. The majority of the companies responding to the survey used in this study were from Kelowna (77%), while Penticton, Osoyoos, Peachland, and Salmon Arm made up 13%. So keep in mind that while this report refers to the Okanagan region, the primary source of activity is from the Kelowna market area.

A few of the key takeaways from this report include:

- The total economic impact of the technology industry to the Okanagan is **$1.3 billion** which has grown by 30% since 2013.
- Approximately 7,600 people work in the Okanagan technology community, representing a 16% increase since 2013.
- There are 633 technology businesses in the Okanagan (355 in the Kelowna CMA) or 13% more than in 2013.
- 18% of persons working in the Professional, Scientific and Technical Sector provided computer systems design and related services in the Kelowna CMA.

April 2017 saw construction completed for the Okanagan Centre For Innovation in downtown Kelowna. It was designed to increase collaboration and drive growth in the region's entrepreneurial, innovation and technology sectors. The Centre offers commercial space along with services and support to start-up and early stage companies, community members, non-profits, and social enterprises.

It is hard not to get excited about these results, especially given that technology is a relatively new industry. These growth rates are extremely encouraging and bode well for the continued growth of our local economy.

Table 2 presents data to show the proportion of the labour force employed in goods-producing and service-producing industries, and the proportion of professional, scientific and technical industries involved in computer design and related activities for selected CMAs.

Table 2. Work force statistics for goods and services sectors within CMAs across Canada.

CMA	Goods Producing	Services Producing	% Computer Occupations
Canada	20.9	79.1	21.5
Victoria	11.8	88.2	26.8
Vancouver	15.6	84.4	23.1
Kelowna	20.7	79.3	18.3
Calgary	22.6	77.4	17.0
Edmonton	22.9	77.1	15.5
Regina	17.8	82.2	21.8
Saskatoon	21.1	78.9	12.3
Winnipeg	17.7	82.3	16.9
Toronto	16.1	83.9	25.4
Ottawa	9.1	90.9	31.5
Montreal	16.6	83.4	26.7
Quebec	14.3	85.7	28.2
St. John	24.3	75.7	30.1
Halifax	12.6	87.4	25.0
St. John's	17.9	82.1	16.4

Source: Statistics Canada, 2016 Census of Population, Statistics Canada Catalogue no. 98-400-X2016290.

The reason we have focused on the technology industry is so that people who are contemplating a move to Kelowna can get a sense of the direction that our economy is moving toward, rather than where our economy has been for the last 100 years.

What About the Tourism Industry?

Our first two tables do not show tourism as a specific industry as it is not reported that way by Statistics Canada. Tourism covers so many aspects of an economy that it requires specific study and analysis to determine its economic value to a community.

In March of 2017, Tourism Kelowna released such a study: *Economic Impact of Tourism in Kelowna and the Greater Kelowna Area, BC*. Table 3 is taken from this study and reveals that the total direct and indirect economic impact of tourism to the Kelowna market is almost **$1.3 Billion!** Please note that we have reproduced this data exactly as reported by source. It is suggested that totals do not add up due to rounding.

Table 3. Total economic impact of tourism in Greater Kelowna area, 2016 (wages, GDP & output = $millions)

Impact	Employment		Wages	GDP	Output
	Jobs	FTEs*			
Direct					
Accommodations	2,200	1,600	$70	$100	$160
Other tourism industries[1]	3,900	2,220	$120	$190	$500
Visitor spending[2]	2,250	1,750	$60	$70	$150
Total Direct	**8,350**	**5,570**	**$240**	**$370**	**$810**
Indirect[3]	2,060	1,380	$80	$130	$250
Induced[3]	1,480	990	$50	$120	$180
Grand Total	**11,890**	**7,940**	**$370**	**$620**	**$1,250**

*Denotes fulltime equivalent jobs.

[1]Other tourism industries impact reflects employment attractions, transportation and other supporting businesses and organizations of the tourism sector in the region.

[2]An estimated 2,250 jobs are associated with visitor spending that takes place in the Kelowna area. The level of visitor spending is based on the 2016 Visitor Intercept Survey conducted by InterVISTAS, and includes expenditure on retail, food and beverage and local transportation.

[3]Does not include direct and induced impacts for visitor spending (only for Accommodations and Other Tourism Industries) to mitigate the possibility of double-counting of impacts. Totals may not add up due to rounding.

We decided to try to put the importance of tourism to our economy into relative perspective so that readers can better understand its importance. We prepared Table 4 to show how much is spent by tourists in 15 major Canadian cities. We were then able to come up with the amount visitors spent annually per resident (per capita) so that we can see how Kelowna compares.

Table 4. Tourist spending per capita of major CMAs.

Census Metropolitan Areas (CMA's)	Annual Visitor Expenditures ($000) 2015	CMA Pop. (000's)	Annual $ Per Capita
Kelowna	**696,227**	**198.3**	**3511**
St. Catharines-Niagara	1,291,018	411.7	3136
St. John's	440,982	217.5	2028
Quebec City	1,608,529	807.2	1993
Victoria	656,280	370.9	1769
Halifax	733,219	425.9	1722
Regina	374,556	247.2	1516
Edmonton	1,880,918	1,392.6	1351
Ottawa-Gatineau	1,808,992	1,351.1	1339
London	668,764	512.4	1305
Calgary	1,592,217	1,469.3	1084
Vancouver	2,540,193	2,548.7	997
Winnipeg	756,043	811.9	931
Toronto	5,490,012	6,242.3	879
Montreal	3,106,778	4,093.8	759

Source: StatsCan Travel Survey of Residents of Canada - CANSIM Table 426-0027.

As you can see, Kelowna ranked number one, which supports two conclusions. First, Kelowna is a much sought-after destination for tourists and, second, those tourists contribute significantly to our local economy.

CHAPTER 37

EMPLOYMENT SITUATION

The most common economic indicator used to understand comparative employment levels is the unemployment rate of a given market. On a national scale, full employment is reached when the unemployment rate is at about 5% or lower.

Will I be Able to Find a Job in Kelowna?

Table 1 compares Kelowna's January 2017/18 seasonally adjusted unemployment rate to a few other Census Metropolitan Areas. Kelowna's unemployment rate dropped 1.1 points over 2017, but remained above the national (5.9%) and BC (4.8%) averages.

Table 1. January year-over-year unemployment rates, seasonally adjusted (3 month moving average).

	2017	2018
Victoria	4.6	3.9
Vancouver	5.0	4.1
Kelowna	**7.6**	**6.5**
Calgary	9.9	7.6
Regina	5.4	4.4
Winnipeg	6.5	5.7
Thunder Bay	6.2	5.8
Toronto	7.0	5.9
Montreal	6.7	5.8
Halifax	6.1	6.8

St. John's	9.8	8.4
B.C.	**5.5**	**4.8**
Canada	**6.7**	**5.9**

Source: Statistics Canada, CANSIM, tables 282-00135 and 282-0087.

The improvement in the unemployment rate in Kelowna during 2017 indicates finding a job is getting easier, depending upon one's education, experience, and the industry chosen. In fact, according to an October 2017 Business Walk survey led by the Central Okanagan Economic Development Commission (COEDC), of 221 businesses in the Kelowna CMA, 78% reported their businesses as growing. According to the Central Okanagan Economic Development Commission's 2017 4th quarter report, job postings were up 29% and 15,576 jobs were posted during 2017.

What Types of Employees are Needed?

In June of 2014, the Central Okanagan Economic Development Commission (COEDC) commissioned R.A. Malatest & Associates Ltd. to do a study of the local employment situation. This study is called Growing in the *Okanagan 2020 Labour Market Outlook*. It details the key findings associated with the Labour Market Study completed for the Okanagan Region (OR), with specific attention to the North, Central and Okanagan-Similkameen Regional Districts.

A few of the key findings of this very extensive and informative report include the following:

- *A large number of new hires will require a post-secondary education.* Over the next six years more than two-thirds of new hires will require some form of post-secondary education, requiring between 37,796 and 50,345 individuals with an advanced education.
- *The ability of the local labour force to fill vacancies is limited.* Given the current education profile of residents in the Okanagan, it would appear that employers may experience difficulty in hiring

individuals who have the appropriate level of education, as almost one-half (45%) of current residents do not have any education or training beyond high school.

- *Employers will require significant numbers of "new" workers in the next six years.* Overall, employers expect that the region's labour force will grow by approximately 18.5% during the next six years. In addition, Okanagan employers will have additional hiring demands required to fill positions vacated by retiring workers and/or workers who are leaving the region. Total new hires for the region are estimated to be in excess of 75,000 workers by the year 2020.

- *Current labour force growth is insufficient to meet regional labour force needs.* Population growth and current migration levels are sufficient to cover between 52.3% and 69.4% of all new hires. Current net migration to the region is required to double or triple to meet labour market demands.

It appears that these results provide good news for future Kelowna job-seekers, especially those with post-secondary education.

In terms of what Okanagan employers are looking for presently and into the future, the same report reveals the top 'difficult to hire' occupations in each of five industries. In other words, there will likely be many more job vacancies in these occupations than there will be workers available to fill them.

1. *Manufacturing* - Welders and Related Machine Operators; Structural Metal and Plate Work Fabricators and Fitters; Machinists and Machining and Tooling Inspectors.

2. *Wholesale and Retail Trade* - Retail Salespersons and Sales Clerks; Cashiers; Heavy-Duty Equipment Mechanics.

3. *Finance and Insurance* - Other Financial Officers; Insurance Agents and Brokers; Sales Representatives – Wholesale Trade (Non-Technical).

4. *Professional, Scientific, and Technical Services* - Computer Programmers and Interactive Media Developers; Technical Sales Specialists; Computer Network Technicians.

5. *Accommodation and Food Services* - Cooks; Food Counter Attendants, Kitchen Helpers, and Related Occupations; Light Duty Cleaners.

According to the results of the 2017 COEDC Business Walk mentioned earlier, recruitment and retention of staff continues to be a barrier to growth. Of the businesses surveyed, 41% reported difficulty filling positions regardless of the business sector listed above.

By way of confirmation, we see that the *Economic Impact of the Okanagan Tech Sector: 2015 Edition,* referred to in our previous chapter, states "lack of qualified talent" as the number one barrier to growth. This coincides with the employment gap findings in industry number 4 above. The bottom line for skilled people who are looking for a job in the tech industry – consider Kelowna, you will be welcomed with open arms.

How Much Will I be Paid?

The closest we could come to answering this question for the Kelowna market was to compile data encompassing a larger geographic area referred to as the Thompson-Okanagan (Table 2). While this information is not as specific as one might desire, it should provide a reasonable idea of local wages.

Table 2. Comparative median wages ($/hr.) Thompson-Okanagan vs Canada as of September, 2017.

Occupation	Median Wages Thompson-Okanagan	Median Wages Canada
Food and Beverage Server	11.35	10.85
Retail Salesperson	12.25	12.00

Customer Financial Service Representative	17.26	17.95
Construction Labourer	18.00	20.00
Office Manager	22.24	23.50
Dental Assistant (Certified)	24.00	21.50
Nurse	40.19	36.00
Plumber	25.00	29.00
Electrician	28.00	29.70
Information Systems Analysts and Consultants	38.46	38.46
Computer Programmers & Interactive Media Developers	38.46	34.62

Source: Government of Canada via www.jobbank.gc.ca.

The job market in Kelowna is definitely improving, according to the latest data that we were able to uncover. Employment is up, job postings are up, and the vast majority of business owners are optimistic about the future.

Admittedly, we are not economists; however, when it comes to the job market in the Kelowna area, it seems that opportunities lay at two extremes. Employers have great difficulty filling very low and very high skill level positions, leaving fewer opportunities in the mid-range. Unfortunately, this is where most of the labour force lives, leaving us with a relatively high unemployment rate.

We recommend that before making a move, job seekers proceed with cautious optimism, coupled with extensive job market research.

CHAPTER 38

BUSINESS CLIMATE

Let us start with the exciting news. In October of 2016, the Canadian Federation of Independent Business (CFIB) named Kelowna as the Top Entrepreneurial City in all of Canada. Now this is a big deal and we'll explain why in a moment. 2016 was the ninth annual look at what entrepreneurial characteristics Canada's largest cities possess. Having read the entire report we can see that the CFIB put a significant amount of thought and effort into determining which cities excelled in each of their 14 criteria. In total, 121 cities were studied, and Kelowna competed in the group with populations greater than 150,000. They used Census Metropolitan Areas for these larger centres, and the top 10 placements are shown in Table 1.

Table 1. Top 10 overall scores, major cities (CMA pop.>150,000).

2016 Ranking	Major City	Score (/100)	2015 Ranking
1	**Kelowna**	**72.0**	**2**
2	Toronto periphery	69.1	5
3	Barrie	68.8	7
4	Guelph	64.8	6
5	Sherbrooke	64.5	11
6	Calgary periphery	63.5	1
6	Victoria	63.5	16
8	Vancouver periphery	62.6	8
9	Montreal periphery	61.2	34
9	Abbotsford-Mission	61.2	14

Kelowna obviously excelled in most of the categories or we wouldn't have won, however we would like to highlight a few of the areas where Kelowna excelled most. We would also like to point out that these highlights are in the more objective and perhaps more meaningful categories.

- Growth in number of business establishments - 1.9% from June, 2015 to May, 2016
- Number of business establishments per capita - 3.8 per 100 residents
- Number of self-employed - 15.1% of total employed
- Building permits - 8.6% of the total number of business establishments
- Full-time hiring - 25.4% of respondents said yes

The employee data displayed in Figure 1 is from the *City of Kelowna Official Community Plan Indicators Report – 2016*. The trend line is quite encouraging as it suggests continued job growth, the lifeblood of any economy.

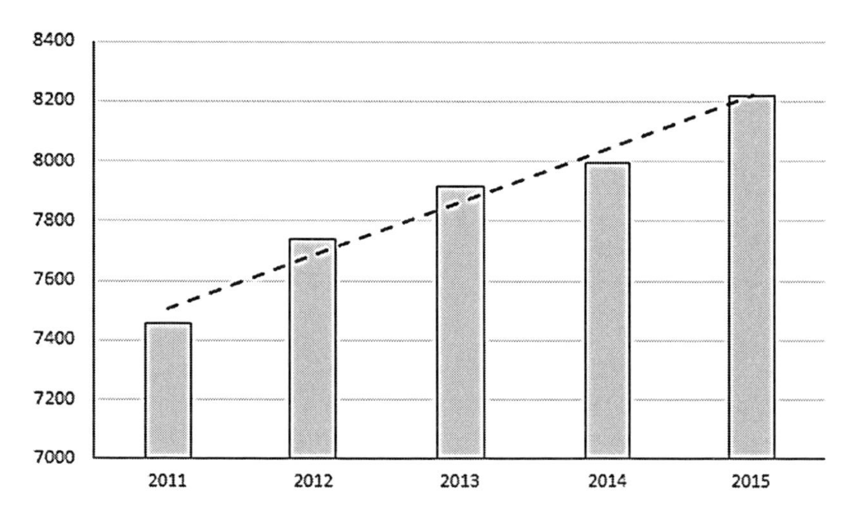

Figure 1. Number of businesses with employees in Kelowna (CMA).

This is pretty exciting stuff, in our humble opinion, and it all bodes well for the future growth of our city. This leads to why we think these results are such a big deal. Economic growth does not happen overnight. It can take a long time for critical mass and infrastructure to develop in order to provide a base from which businesses can grow from small entities into medium and large enterprises. Perhaps the above results are proving that the foundation for rapid growth is in place and that Kelowna can look forward to a prosperous and growing economy in the years to come. We believe so.

Useful Business Briefs

- *Size of Trade Area:* The Central Okanagan Economic Development Commission states, "Kelowna and the Central Okanagan is the largest trading area in the interior of British Columbia, representing a base of approximately 520,000 customers."
- *2018 Corporate Income Tax:* British Columbia's general corporate income tax rate is 12%, among the lowest in Canada. The small business tax rate in 2018 was 2.5%, tied for lowest in Canada. Our combined federal-provincial rate is 27%, among the lowest in G7 countries.
- *Lease Costs:* As with most real estate opportunities, cost and demand can vary greatly by location. The averages below are offered as a guide to compare against your current market.

	$ Cost / ft.^{2}	Vacancy Rate %
Retail	21.50	3.29
Office	18.00	9.11
Industrial	12.00	1.82

Source: Colliers International - Kelowna Research and Forecast Report Q4, 2017.

- *Best of the Worst for Cost of Doing Business:* Since 1996, KPMG has produced a study called *Competitive Alternatives - KPMG's Guide to International Business Locations Costs.* The 2016 edition compares 26 location-sensitive business cost factors for more than 100 individual cities in 10 countries. Seventeen Canadian cities were included in the study. In Table 3, business costs are expressed as a percentage index, with the United States being assigned a baseline index of 100. An index below 100 indicates lower costs than the US. An index over 100 indicates higher costs than the US. For example, an index result of 95.0 represents a 5.0 percent cost advantage relative to the US base.

Table 3. Percentage of cost of doing business among selected Pacific Region cities (base US 100.0).

1	**Kelowna, BC**	**85.5**
2	Vancouver, BC	86.2
3	Boise, ID	94.3
4	Spokane, WA	96.0
5	Portland, OR	97.6
6	Las Vegas, NV	98.0
7	Sacramento, CA	98.5
8	Riverside-San Bernardino, CA	98.5
9	San Diego, CA	99.9
10	Seattle, WA	100.8
11	Los Angeles, CA	100.8
12	Honolulu, HI	103.9
13	San Francisco, CA	104.5

Source: KPMG's Guide to International Business Locations Costs 2016.

The KPMG study states:

The Pacific Region of the US and Canada represents the most costly region in this study. Business costs for the two Canadian cities in this region are slightly above the Canadian average (of 85.4), while average costs for the 12 US cities compared exceed the US base. Only eight cities in the study have business costs above the US baseline, with five being in the Pacific Region.

Advice Column

We are relatively comfortable in offering our insights and opinions on this topic as we have owned and operated quite a few businesses in the Kelowna area for more than twenty-five years. These included ventures in the retail, wholesale, manufacturing, real estate and consulting industries. Based on this practical and hands-on experience, we would like to offer our entrepreneurial readers a few points of advice.

- *Kelowna is a sought-after destination with a transitioning job market.* This means that high paying jobs are few, and many cashed-up entrepreneurs from other cities are on the constant look-out for business opportunities in our area. They are often experienced business people looking for a lifestyle change. This phenomenon just adds to an already competitive marketplace.

- *Check your attitude at the door.* Personal experience has shown that many entrepreneurs who have come from larger cities display some degree of arrogance. They are going to teach the little city people how to do business right. Cracking a new market without a business network is tough enough, so try to cooperate, not criticize.

- *Do your homework.* There is no better way to ensure your success in business than to do an effective job of your market research before you contemplate a start-up, or even the purchase of an existing business. The high turnover rate in the Kelowna restaurant industry is a testament to this suggestion.

- *Kelowna is business friendly.* Obstacles to opening a business are no more challenging here than in other centres. In fact, the number of business support organizations are many and of high quality. A few examples include:

  - ☑ Central Okanagan Economic Development Commission
  - ☑ Accelerate Okanagan
  - ☑ Community Futures

☑ Women's Enterprise Centre

☑ Small Business BC

- *Consider picking up a copy* of ***How Much Money Can I Make? Proven Strategies for Starting, Managing and Exiting a Canadian Small Business*** by Tim Young. Yes, this is a shameless plug, but it does cover eight businesses that were operated in the Kelowna market, so it is quite relevant for those thinking of starting or buying a business here.

In closing, one simply has to take a walk downtown to feel the buzz. New buildings are going up to accommodate more and more businesses, and the employees who work there want to be close to their workplace, shopping, nightlife and the waterfront. The energy is present and the next few years will definitely be an exciting time for the business growth of the millennial generation in Kelowna.

See Chapter 40 for our trusted business contact offering a discount on business services.

PART FOUR

Okay, What's The Catch? . . . Every City Has Its Challenges!

"THE PESSIMIST SEES THE DIFFICULTY IN EVERY OPPORTUNITY; AN OPTIMIST SEES THE OPPORTUNITY IN EVERY DIFFICULTY."
WINSTON CHURCHILL

CHAPTER 39

TEN THINGS YOU SHOULD KNOW BEFORE YOU MOVE TO KELOWNA

It is difficult to criticize the city that we love so much. Having said this, we must be true to one of the main objectives of this book which is to inform our readers about the potential drawbacks of living in Kelowna. We believe that the most informed newcomers will become the happiest residents as they will be more prepared for, and accepting of, the possible challenges they may encounter.

Our joys are many and our regrets are few. Kelowna is a great place to live; however, like every city, it does have its downsides.

1. Catch 22 on the Weather

Kelowna is one of the sunniest places in Canada, spring through fall. Come winter, however, the picture changes dramatically. Our research reveals that Kelowna is ranked among the cloudiest Canadian cities during the months of November through January.

Our second year in Kelowna had us dreading the coming winter months as it can really have a negative effect on one's psyche. Back home on the Prairies, it may have been

bone chillingly cold, but the bright sunshine seemed to compensate and evoke a cheerier outlook. We eventually got over the depressing feelings that dull skies can cause, but we know many who couldn't. We should also mention that the more sedentary one is, the more likely one will succumb to feelings of unhappiness. We suggest an active lifestyle is a great way to fight the winter-time blues.

To end this point on a positive note, we'd just like to say that, over the last 25 winters, there has never been a need to plug in our vehicles.

2. Traffic can Test One's Patience

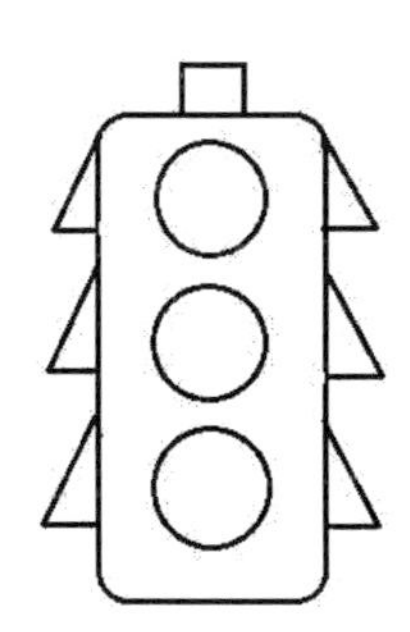

Of the two highways (33 and 97) passing through the city, Highway 97 is the much busier and more congested route. From the south end of West Kelowna to the north end of Kelowna, Highway 97 carries commercial, public transit, local and tourist traffic through a continuous strip mall of commercial and retail developments. The 2016 census revealed 81% of Kelowna's labour force drove to work, 11% and 8% above the provincial and national averages, respectively.

After crossing the floating bridge into Kelowna, drivers face 16 traffic lights along the 11.6 km (7.2 mi.) distance to the last light as you leave the city. That is one light every 0.7 km (0.45 mi.). We wondered if these lights are even synchronized, however our inquiry to highway engineers was not responded to by the time we went to print.

3. Crime is an Issue

Sometimes facts get in the way of a good story. That's just reality and it would be irresponsible of us not to reiterate that our community has a higher than average crime rate. Refer to Chapter 15 for a more complete discussion on this topic. If you were to ask us if we feel safe on the streets of Kelowna, the answer would be a "hell, yes"! The truth is, however, that we live in safe neighbourhoods, we don't go out carousing until the early morning hours, we make sure our homes and vehicles are secured, and we use common sense to avoid conflicts with less law-abiding individuals.

4. Securing Employment May Be A Challenge

Chapter 37 on employment provides enough data to suggest that it would be a good idea to find a job before relocating to Kelowna. Our current unemployment rate is somewhat high which makes the job market competitive, especially for those with lesser skills and education.

5. Lack of Affordable Housing

High home prices, coupled with the extremely low rental vacancy rate, as described in Chapter 14, has resulted in tremendous challenges for newcomers, especially those with lower incomes. While this phenomenon is primarily market-driven, and should eventually revert to more normalized levels, local government seems to be doing its part to alleviate the chronic shortage of affordable rental accommodation in the city.

6. Sporadic Potable Water Supply

If you are looking to buy a property with water provided by either the Black Mountain Irrigation District, the Glenmore-Ellison Improvement District, or the South East Kelowna Irrigation District, be aware that you may have cloudy or brownish water, especially in the spring. People in these areas needing a higher level of protection may want to boil the water before drinking.

7. Prefer to see Deer in 'Your' Backyard

Chapter 24 described the growing problem of urbanized deer in Kelowna and area. Deer can be a nuisance to gardeners, a threat to dog-walkers, and a hazard to drivers. In addition, there is no 'official' help on the horizon to eliminate or minimize this presence.

8. What's That Foul Smell and What's That Noise?

Chapter 5 describes how 40% of the land within Kelowna is in the Agricultural Land Reserve (ALR). This means that there are many residential properties bordering active cropping, livestock, vineyard or orchard operations. Smells and noises from normal farm practices do not stop at property lines.

During May and June, one may be exposed to 'chemical' smells as growers apply necessary pesticides to protect their crops. In addition, the noise of tractors, sprayers and propane cannon explosions to scare birds away from cherry orchards (July - August) and vineyards (September - October) are prevalent. You may hear helicopters hovering over a cherry orchard after a rain to dry the ripening fruit so it won't split. You may also be exposed to offensive odours throughout the year if living next door to an intensive livestock operation.

9. Grasping, but Watch that Driveway

Living on the hillsides around Kelowna provides remarkable views of the City and Okanagan Lake. Hillside properties usually mean a sloping driveway down or up to the garage. Wet snow that freezes onto the surface can make it nearly impossible to safely navigate a steep driveway. We don't know how many garage doors have been accidentally punched in, or how many close calls or crashes have occurred as a result of out-of-control vehicles or toboggans sliding onto streets. This is just something to keep in mind when choosing your new home.

10. Smoke Gets in Your Eyes (and Throat and Lungs and...)

Although Kelowna is not the only city to be impacted by smoky air from forest fires during the summer, we felt you should be aware that this can pose a challenge to children, the elderly, and people with respiratory problems. Most of western North America experienced many very smoky days in 2017.

According to information provided March 2016 in the Okanagan Adaptation Strategies report which describes potential risks posed by climate change to agriculture in the region, the Okanagan Valley will see increasingly warmer and drier summers. As a result, the region will experience larger and more frequent wildfires, and an extension of the wildfire season. This will lead to more days with smoke in the air and possibly at greater concentrations for longer periods. During the summer of 2017, air quality in Kelowna posed a health risk on 25 days; this is significantly greater than the average 4.5 days per summer since 2003. On the plus side, the frequency of future fires should diminish as current forests are lost to fires.

There you have it. These are some challenges that most Kelownians can identify with. All cities have downsides, and we trust that sharing ours will help you to make a more informed decision about moving here.

PART FIVE

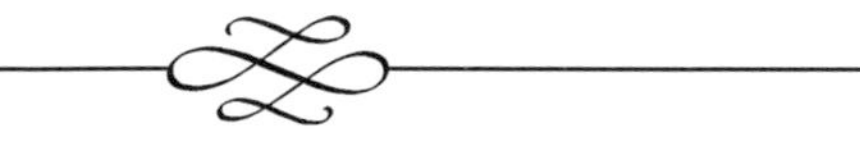

Business People You Can Trust!

"IF PEOPLE LIKE YOU, THEY'LL LISTEN TO YOU,
BUT IF THEY TRUST YOU,
THEY'LL DO BUSINESS WITH YOU."
ZIG ZIGLAR

CHAPTER 40

A FEW GREAT BUSINESSES TO HELP YOU SETTLE IN

Our list of referrals is a valuable asset to all newcomers to the Kelowna area. This list includes businesses who are known to have provided above-average customer service to Kelowna clients for more than five years. Each name is that of the business owner, or their designate, who has supported the publication of this book. Unless otherwise noted, all referrals listed here have agreed to offer a minimum discount of 10% off the cost of either their goods or their services, or both, depending upon the type of business. This book is your coupon, and will be honored upon presentation. In some cases, this offer may be limited to one discount per printed book.

- **A-1 Boarding Kennels**
  Alexis & Paul Furer (Owners)
  3755 Gordon Drive, Kelowna, BC V1W 4M8
  Telephone: 250-763-2202
  Email: Boardin_on_gordon@shaw.ca
  Website: www.A1boardingkennels.ca

- **AmeriSpec Inspection Services**
  Murray Klingbeil (Owner)
  PO Box 20035, Kelowna, BC V1Y 9H2
  Telephone: 250-763-0822
  Email: okanagan@amerispec.ca
  Website: www.homeinspectionkelowna.ca

- **Business Finders Canada**
  Nelson Bayford (Professional Business & Commercial Real Estate Broker)
  1652 Pandosy Street - Kelowna, BC V1Y 1PZ
  Tel: 778-215-6500
  Fax: 778-484-3232
  Email: nelson@businessfinderscanada.com
  Website: www.businessfinderscanada.com

- **Comfort Tech Heating & Cooling Ltd.**
  Terri Wilkinson (Owner)
  1750 Springfield Road, Kelowna, BC V1Y 5V6
  Telephone: 250-258-5713
  Email: greatservice@comforttech.ca
  Website: www.comforttech.ca

- **Creative Mortgage Corp.**
  Trish Balaberde (Mortgage Broker)
  #200 – 1505 Harvey Avenue, Kelowna, BC V1Y 6G1
  Telephone: 250-470-8324
  Email: trishb@creativemortgage.ca
  Website: www.kelownahomemortgages.ca

- **Forman Automotive & Transmission**
  Mike Forman (Owner)
  5 – 1691 Powick Road, Kelowna, BC V1X 4L1
  Telephone: 250-862-398

❖ **GTA Architecture Ltd.**[1]
Garry Tomporowski (Principal)
243-1889 Springfield Road, Kelowna, BC V1Y 5V5
Telephone: 250-979-1668
Email: garry@gtarch.ca
Website: www.gtarch.ca

❖ **Kelowna Inn & Suites**
1070 Harvey Avenue, Kelowna, BC V1Y 8S4
Telephone: 250-762-2533
Email: reservations@kelownainn.com
Website: www.kelownainnandsuites.com

❖ **Make Their Day Services** - House cleaning and more
Paulette Gill (Owner)
Kelowna, BC
Telephone: 778-760-4579
Email: maketheirdayservices@gmail.com
Website: www.maketheirday.ca

❖ **Rory Fader Piano Tuning**
Rory Fader B.Mus., RPT
Kelowna, BC
Telephone: 250-864-1528
Email: rfader@telus.net
Website: www.roryfaderpianotuning.ca

❖ **Sunshine Pools & Spas**[2]
Ken Reid (Owner)
123-1889 Springfield Road, Kelowna, BC V1Y 5V5
Telephone: 250-717-8381
Email: info@sunshinepools.ca
Website: www.sunshinepools.ca

- **The UPS Store**
  Mark Ledwon (Owner)
  101-1865 Dilworth Drive, Kelowna, BC V1Y 9T1
  Telephone: 250-860-6215
  Email: store40@theupsstore.ca
  Website: www.theupsstore.ca

- **Total E'clips SalonSpa**
  Kathie Jones (Owner)
  #107 – 3957 Lakeshore Road, Kelowna, BC V1W 1V3
  Telephone: 250-764-8117
  Email: info@totale-clips.com
  Website: www.totale-clips.com

- **Wiener's Plumbing & Irrigation**
  Wayne Schaeffer (Owner)
  1186 High Road, Kelowna, BC V1Y 7B1
  Telephone: 250-862-8886
  Email: wienerplumbing@shaw.ca
  Website: www.wienersplumbingandirrigation.com

[1] Offering preferred customer status in lieu of discount.

[2] Discount may exclude pool construction.

In closing, we invite readers to contact us if you have further questions about Kelowna life. We can be reached via our website at www.movingtokelowna.net.